Once a Shooter

Once a Shooter

REDEMPTION OF A HIGH SCHOOL GUNMAN

A PERSONAL TESTIMONY BY

TJ STEVENS WITH JOHN DRIVER

SALEM
BOOKS

an imprint of Regnery Publishing

ISBN: 978-1-68451-019-1
Ebook ISBN: 978-1-68451-043-6

Library of Congress Control Number:2019956084

Published in the United States by
Salem Books, an imprint of
Regnery Publishing
A Division of Salem Media Group
300 New Jersey Ave NW
Washington, DC 20001

www.Regnery.com

Manufactured in the United States of America

10 9 8 7 6 5 4 3 2 1

Books are available in quantity for promotional or premium use. For information on discounts and terms, please visit our website: www.Regnery.com.

Contents

Introduction

There have been times in my life that I have had to hide. The reasons, as you will soon discover, were tragically beyond my control. At times, I was hiding from real, imminent danger. But for far longer—decades, that is—I have been hiding in plain sight somewhere else altogether, and it's not been from danger.

Shame has been my hiding place.

The story you are about to read is one I would really rather you never hear, or at least, the part of me that still longs to live in the shadows doesn't want you to hear it. But I am writing it anyway because I know it needs to be told. There are too many others out there hiding in the shadows of danger or in the shadows of shame—or both. I am writing for them, even if it means writing about my worst moments in life.

But even more than them, I am writing for the One who has never lost sight of me, even in the darkest corners of my story. One step at a time and in varying degrees, He has brought me out of shame and into sonship. My redemption has been a slow-moving fog of grace—the beautiful kind of fog you see hanging low and dense over serene mountain streams like the ones winding through the woods around my home in Winchester, Virginia.

But my story is anything but serene. There are valid reasons for my shame, so much so that when I penned the first draft of this book, the editors commented that I wrote too much about the shame I have felt over the years. They didn't mean that it is inconsequential, but that at some point, saying it over and over again might detract from the flow of the story. So while I will mention it again in places, I am trying to take their advice and just tell you up front that, for over thirty-five years, I have experienced intense, gut-wrenching shame over the actions of my youth. So when you're reading my story and the realization of who is writing this book hits you again, just know that I get it. I don't feel entitled, and I do feel completely unworthy.

I don't want myself or anyone else to benefit from this story simply because it is interesting and will hit some of the "hot buttons" of our modern culture. I actually started writing my thoughts down over seven years ago. I was even approached by someone about a movie deal, but I turned it down because something just didn't feel right. I want this story told the right way and for the right reasons—and I will explain what I think those reasons are in the pages to come.

I know what it feels like to hide. Maybe you do too. This book is yet another step I'm taking out of the shadows, and my deepest hope is that it may brighten the shadows for someone else who thinks no one can see them. Take it from one of the dark ones: it's not true.

There is light, no matter who you are, where you've been, or what you've done … let my dark story show you what I mean.

CHAPTER 1

Light Unexpected

*O*nce *a shooter* walked alone through the front doors of a normal, unsuspecting high school in Burke, Virginia. He was young. Troubled. Tormented. Drowning in a cavernous darkness so deep that light itself seemed to have ceased to exist. It is an all-too-familiar story these days. After all, *once a shooter* enters a school or another public space, nothing but darkness follows.

Or does it?

Relentless

Stage lights can be blinding. Oddly enough, I should know. I've seen a lot of them. I say, "oddly enough" because it is truly odd that a guy like me—or more specifically, the guy who is me—would ever find himself experiencing any sort of spotlight, stage light, or quite frankly, the light of day.

Nevertheless, I've seen some crazy light.

I've sat on movie and television sets under bright lights, talking about my life, my horrible choices, and the completely unimaginable story that followed. *CBS. CityGate Films. I Am Second.* And many more. I've also sat under the gently swaying light of a restaurant booth across from a reporter from *The Washington Post*, reluctantly telling him the details of a story that, quite honestly, people unsuccessfully tried to get me to talk about for over three decades.

Maybe that is why I have changed my name five times—trying to avoid this light.

But now, somehow, you are reading my words, perhaps by the florescent light of some airport terminal or the soft light of your bedside lamp. This particular fact—this light that is bringing us together now in the pages of this book—is nothing less than shocking.

In many ways, it seems as if this light has been chasing me my whole life, and there were plenty of times that I ran from it—hard. Even so, it has always remained hot on my trail, trying to catch me—longing not just to expose me, but also to do something mysteriously more.

There was a time when the light became so bright that it illuminated downtown streets in metro areas like Washington, DC, and New York City to reveal a completely unknown young man (because he was actually concealing his identity at the time) who had spent his short life up to that point immersed in the blackest of darkness. Yet he had become an actor in an internationally acclaimed live rendition of the Passion, performing before millions of people from all across the world. Celebrities and cynics. Presidents and paupers. Leaders and losers.

And at the very center of this diverse group of onlookers, the character this unknown actor was portraying happened to be Jesus Christ himself—played by the biggest loser of all. Even with so much bright light all around, no one knew who he was—who *I* was. In fact, for over thirty-seven years, no one other than my wife and close family has ever really known exactly who I am. As you hear the details of my story, you'll probably understand why. However, I doubt that you will be able to logically comprehend how this light has pursued me, even into the darkest of corners.

As I reveal pieces of this story, you may not like what you hear—and I don't mean just the difficult parts of the story—that is, the darkness. Yes, those are indeed dark and disturbing, so much so that I still often cringe when I tell them. I am not proud of them—not in the least. I do not share them for the sake of notoriety, financial gain, or fame. In fact, I wish they had never happened and that my name was not attached to this book. But I also wish that there weren't so many other stories just like this one emerging seemingly every other week in the news. In this sense, the dark parts of my story may be somehow tragically familiar to you.

Yet even though the darkness may be difficult, it may actually be the light that you won't want to see. Why? Because I'm not going to hold back on exactly what has happened to me. It won't be pretty, and it might not fit neatly into a culturally or politically correct box. There won't be neat bows or rounded edges. I have no excuse for what I chose to do, but there is a *backstory*—especially my childhood—that leads up to my worst moment—a *story* that may take you *aback*.

Furthermore, you may not agree with, much less believe, other aspects of the story I'm going to tell you, which is your choice. You may be tempted to roll your eyes at various parts, especially when my story crosses into the supernatural, which it sometimes does. We have a tendency to do that these days— roll our eyes at the supernatural, even as the darkest elements of evil go on killing rampages all around us that mirror the very supernatural elements by which we love to be scared in horror movies, books, or video games.

We call those things "fake." "Mere entertainment." *Not "the real world."* But then we turn on the news and see the exact same things actually happening *in the real world*—and still most of us reject the role of any sort of supernatural elements in these disasters. The tragic reality is that most of the people at the helm of these disastrous events do not live to tell about it—and if they do, they are dismissed outright for the madmen they obviously are.

But what if one of these madmen came back from the brink, regaining his right mind?

You see, I was dead, but I lived to tell about it. Hear me: I was dead and buried. A Coward. A Failure. A young man with pain piling upon pain. A time bomb just waiting to det- onate, set off by the smallest of occurrences in my pathetic life. I was the most dangerous kind of madman, hiding in plain sight within the Trojan horse of a high school.

And yet I lived to tell about it. Perhaps you will conclude that I have no right to tell about it, much less to live. I actually couldn't agree more. I don't deserve to live or to tell this story. I actually tried to accept—even create—both of these realities by attempting to end my own life, and when that didn't pan out, to try to hide my story.

But the light has proven surprisingly more relentless than the darkness.

Perhaps you see the images of today's disturbed gunmen, either recently taken out by the bullets of a SWAT team or being led away in shackles on television, and think to yourself, *What is wrong with people these days! These crazed maniacs!*

In essence, we see such people and conclude that they are beyond the reach of reason, much less redemption. *Once a shooter*, always a shooter. I would wholeheartedly agree with this assessment if it were not for the shocking fact that I myself have somehow become the very living proof that this is not always true. I was a dead man walking in a darkness that will be shocking for you to behold, but this persistent, mysterious light refused to concede to my shadows or to accept my fate of death as the final word in my story.

This is my story. You see, I was *once a shooter*.

Dark Whispers

I was merely eighteen years old. Though I couldn't see it at the time, my life was really just getting started. But from my twisted vantage point of pain, shame, and rage, I had reached the point where I believed that suicide was my only way out. I was imploding, ready to end it all.

It was about 2 a.m. on November 10, 1982, and I was alone in my bedroom, engulfed in total darkness. The night sky outside my window was obviously dark, but it was nothing compared to the darkness of the mind and soul within me. It's easy to simply refer to the metaphorical "darkness" and miss its real punch, so it might be more helpful to use the word "pain."

A deep, tormenting pain had gripped my total being, the culmination of years of emotional disintegration. Later, I will share in greater detail about the journey that had led me to this shadowy moment, but for now, it suffices to say that my lingering state of being had led me into this pitch-black night of the soul. And yet strangely, I felt a sense of evil serenity. I had become like a zombie: I was breathing, yet I was already dead on the inside. This inner death cried out for symmetry ... for the rest of me to follow suit. It was time to die and be done with it all. Truthfully, I could not see any other way out.

The pain was just too great to bear—building up inside me for as long as I could remember.

I began carefully loading high-powered .22-250 shells into the rifle I had received for my sixteenth birthday. I put them in one by one, feeling the power and potential of each round as it made a metallic *clack* after insertion. Once it was completely loaded, I disengaged the safety. Then, awkwardly finagling the firearm to do something it was not designed to do, I was finally able to place the end of the barrel in my mouth. This was it—the end was finally here. My hands were shaking, and I waited for what was to follow.

But instead of the deafening blast of a single shot from a fully loaded rifle, I suddenly heard a different sound. It startled me because I was completely alone, in every sense of the word. Where was it coming from? The best I can say is that it came from the darkness itself.

"You want real peace?" the voice whispered loudly.

Obviously, since my death was already about to happen, the voice had an additional, more sinister purpose in speaking out of the darkness to interrupt my impending suicide.

"If you do this my way," the voice continued, "I'll give you real peace. We'll show them."

All at once, the directive became clear—if I would go and kill others first and then kill myself afterward, I'd finally be at rest. I know this sounds absolutely insane, mainly because it is. Even so, in my dark world of a cowardly self-pity and loneliness, my mind was being filled with evil. My ultimate goal—and indeed the voice's ultimate goal for me as well—was my own death. But in the process of destroying my own life, I would now also become the vehicle of a great and destructive deception—the lie I had bought that said killing others would make killing myself make even more sense. In that dark moment, I gave in to the whims of this darker voice. I made the choice to allow it to control my mind, my body, and my soul. After all, what did it matter?

I was already dead anyway.

After a sleepless night of endless agony and personal torment, being on time for school the next morning was of little importance. Besides, I needed to wait long enough to let everyone get inside the building and settled into their routine.

So I spent the morning packing additional rounds of ammunition into the many pockets of a long winter coat. Darkness now covered me both inside and out.

Approximately eight hours had transpired since my nightmarish decision the night before, but I remained just as stiffly resolute, hell-bent on wreaking havoc on as many people as possible, including myself. At 10:17 a.m. on the morning of November 10, I walked into Lake Braddock Secondary High School in Burke, Virginia, wearing my long winter coat, which concealed my loaded rifle and extra ammo.

When I was about two feet inside the front doors that had securely shut behind me, I opened fire into the main hallway of the school.

HOSTAGE

We've all seen it on the news: the unthinkable becomes reality in one of the very locations that should be most safe and secure … until it's not. I wonder how many times someone watching just such a scene unfold on television has turned to the person next to them and said something like, "What in the world can be going through that crazy person's head that could cause them to do such a thing?"

It's a valid question. And while I can't speak for every school shooter—it's not like we know each other—I do have a tragically unique perspective on what goes through someone's mind in the moment they are wreaking such devastation.

My mind was not on any sort of logical plane. In other words, I wasn't questioning. I wasn't second-guessing.

I wasn't worried about how it would all end. No, I was just shooting … from the hip. I could fire nine rounds with my bolt-action rifle before needing to reload.

The whole environment around me was instantly and completely overwhelmed by my presence—and this only emboldened me all the more. Finally, *I* was in control. The smell of smoke and gunpowder seeped into the fibers of clothes—and seemingly into the fibers of my being. The deafening gunshots made most every other sound disappear—except, that is, the incessant ringing in my ears and the distant screams of women and children. They were screaming and running for their lives. But all I could think was …

Control. Power. Kill.

I walked down the hallway, approaching a row of windows to my left. I was in a frenzy that dominated every other part of my mind, so I took the butt of my gun and began smashing them out. I had no thought or plan, just rage. The rooms on the other side of the windows were filled with faculty and staff. As I busted the windows, they screamed in horror—and with each scream, I fed upon their growing terror.

I was so completely absorbed with the mission of fulfilling my rampage of death and destruction that I did not realize I had sustained a self-inflicted injury—a deep cut on my right hand from the flying, jagged glass of the office wall. Blood was literally pouring from my right hand, but I felt no pain. I was being moved by a force unlike anything I had ever known in my life, being driven to a single end goal: death for myself and for others.

Hundreds of high school students continued to scream and scramble for their lives throughout the hallways. I could see and hear many of them as they scurried for safety.

I broke through the doors of the office where I had smashed the windows and continued shooting. For some unknown reason, I always shot above their heads and never straight into the crowd. As is true of most old school buildings, there were concrete walls and ceilings behind the ceiling tiles. Perhaps I was in a nonsensical trance or perhaps there were other forces at work, but to this day, I do not know how one of the many rounds I recklessly fired into those rooms did not ricochet and injure or kill one of those teachers or students.

After all, I emptied and reloaded my rifle several times.

In my state of rage, I did not realize that the room I had entered was an office area—the only room in the building completely concealed from the outside. It had full concrete ceilings and walls, so there was no way in or out, other than using C4 explosives to blast one's way in. I also didn't realize that in the adjoining room in the back of this area, a woman was hiding in fear for her life. Throughout all that was to come, I never saw her. At gunpoint, I ordered the rest of the teachers to gather on one side of the room.

I had officially taken hostages.

Nine innocent people's lives were now in my powerful, bleeding hands. I had no intent to use them for any survival advantage. I was still completely bent on killing them all and then killing myself.

Then the office phone rang.

It was the SWAT negotiator, a man named Don Grant. His voice on the other end of that phone meant nothing to me at the time, but in the years to come, this opinion would change.

Don asked me about my demands, but I really didn't have any coherent requests, so I just began to spew whatever came to my deranged mind. I said things like, "If you don't give me what I want, then bodies will start lining up down this hallway!" But I never actually told him anything that I really wanted, other than speaking to a few people who included an ex-girlfriend … besides, he couldn't have given me the peace the voice in the darkness had promised me. I hung up the phone.

Soon I could hear the sound of helicopters outside, along with sirens announcing the arrival of many police and emergency vehicles. (*The Washington Post* would later give the number as "eight score.") The press also arrived *en masse*. The other 4,300 people in the building, mostly students, were still in their classrooms and could not leave because no one was completely certain exactly where I was. Their nightmare continued.

At first, I did not converse with the hostages at all. Even so, I still carried on conversations that lasted for many hours—actually, for almost two days. The people in that room were my hostages, but I was being tormented by my own captors.

By midnight, the singular voice had become multiple voices—and they were constantly telling me which hostage to kill first, and so forth and so on. They kept screaming at me that we had a deal and that I was breaking it. The voices became louder and stronger, no matter how much I tried to mollify them.

Death for me was still a foregone conclusion, but somewhere in the melee, I found myself actually trying to pull back from killing the hostages. I began arguing with the voices, demanding to be released from the deal I had made with them to kill these innocent people. But the voices raged back against me violently. I screamed at them, and they at me.

The hostages looked at me like I was a lunatic—and I was. I had lost control and now literally felt possessed by these voices. Even so, there was no excuse for the cowardly acts I was committing because I had chosen this path. I had let these voices in.

The Blinding Light

I deserved death—that much I knew.

All the while, the phone kept incessantly ringing and ringing, so I finally ripped the cord out of the wall in frustration. What I didn't realize was that the negotiator on the other end was my only lifeline—the one who could keep the order to kill me on sight from being given. I left him no choice.

I was raging, screaming obscenities at God, at the voices, and at myself. The voices screamed, "Kill! Kill! Kill!" over and over again as I tried to resist them. This back-and-forth lasted all night.

By the second day, November 11, I could no longer take it. In desperation, I got down on my knees in front of the hostages, loaded another shell into my rifle, placed the butt of the gun on the floor, and positioned the barrel in my mouth for the second time in two days. With the safety off, I put my thumb on the trigger and began to apply pressure so that I could finally end the tortuous onslaught of the voices ... and my own life.

The hostages began to scream and cry. Honestly, they screamed and cried more when I put the gun in my own mouth than when I had pointed it at them. They had a compassionate concern for me, their captor, that I didn't understand. But as I put a bit more pressure on the trigger, a young woman, the school secretary, fell to her knees and began weeping uncontrollably. She rocked back and forth with her hands over her face crying, begging, and praying, "No, no, no ... don't do this! You're just a confused kid! You don't know what you're doing!"

When she did this, I involuntarily pulled the gun out of my mouth and jerked toward her ... almost as if someone had thrown holy water on me during some sort of exorcism. My eyes and face were drenched in tears, so I had significant trouble seeing her clearly, but still I gazed in her direction with the most evil of stares. As she was rocking back and forth, something near her created a reflection that glared—no, pierced—straight into my right eye. It penetrated the darkness of my soul like a spear. The light was reflecting off a gold cross on her necklace, slowly swaying beneath her as she continued to cry on her knees.

In this moment, I felt something that no person expects to feel just before they take their own life—peace. Deep, illogical peace. But something in me had to fiercely resist it, so I fell into another rage. I screamed at the woman, "You! Get out of here!" I knew I couldn't control myself and that I would kill her if she didn't leave because of that cross around her neck. It felt as if I was on fire on the inside … burning as I was confronted by the cross. Some of the hostages were now crying even louder because of my latest escalation.

Then, something miraculous happened. I *saw* something. It was the sleeve of a white robe with a hand. It bore no scars, and I could not see whose it was, but the hand was right next to me. It never touched me. It just waited … for me. It's hard to describe, but when I saw that hand, my soul became aware that I was standing before Grace personified, something a person like me should not encounter. Every voice I had been battling had suddenly hushed. The hand still waited …

Finally, reluctantly, I found myself reaching out to touch it.

CHAPTER 2

The Beginnings of "From There to Here"

My past is something I've been running from my entire adult life. Only in recent years have I felt the not-so-subtle nudge to come out of the shadows and share my story. And though I have much to share (and honestly, much to lose), the very act of talking with people about my history reveals certain patterns. There are certain things most people really seem to want to know.

One of the most common things I hear is, "How did you get from *that* moment to *this* one?" I get it. The scene I just described to you is one of sheer horror—a waking nightmare, above all for the poor victims of my heinous actions. In fact, one of the main reasons I'm writing this book is to acknowledge my inexcusable fault in the whole story. While I am eternally grateful that, inexplicably, no bullets found their way to any of the people in Lake Braddock High School that day, this doesn't mean I didn't inflict a lot of wounds.

Because I did.

Obviously, "sorry" doesn't exactly cut it when you've put innocent people and their loved ones in harm's way … in the worst way. Over the years that have followed that particular day—the day that has defined so much of my life—I have had the opportunity to meet some of the people who were in the school that day and their families. For the most part, they have graciously allowed me to express my deepest sorrow. Some of them have even forgiven me; others, understandably, have not.

But the fact remains that very few people are not at least a little curious about the path that led me from that moment with a gun in my mouth to this one. How does a person see such a drastic change, especially after having sunk so low that there was seemingly no pathway back to the surface? I mean, shooting up a high school is simply something you never come back from. Trust me, those were my exact thoughts as well.

What was done was done, which meant that *I was done* too … or so I thought.

I often think back to an ancient story that is famous mostly because a bunch of pigs collectively careened over a cliff to their deaths. It is a strange story, but for me, the pigs are not the most compelling part—not in the least. The story begins when Jesus gets off a boat on the shores of a town called Gerasen, only to be met by a man who was severely entrenched in his own level of darkness—as deep as it gets. I can relate.

Scripture reveals that,

For a long time he had worn no clothes, and he had not lived in a house but among the tombs. When he saw Jesus, he cried out and fell down before him and said with a loud voice, "What have you to do with me, Jesus, Son of the Most High God? I beg you, do not torment me." For he had commanded the unclean spirit to come out of the man. (For many a time it had seized him. He was kept under guard and bound with chains and shackles, but he would break the bonds and be driven by the demon into the desert.) (Luke 8:27–29 ESV)

This guy called the tombstones his home—a place where he had lived, naked, for years on end—that is, when he wasn't out roaming around naked and aimless in the desert instead. The townspeople were obviously afraid of him, and rightfully so. He was a danger to all of them. They had often tried to take him into custody to protect themselves and their families, but just when they thought they had him completely restrained, he would snap their chains like threads.

To make a long story short, an unlikely hand reached out to him as well. The evil spirits left him and took residence in a herd of pigs—and the rest, as they say, is history of the strangest sort. But again, to me the most compelling part of the story is the description of the man after the whole crazy event has gone down.

The townspeople—who all knew their criminally disturbed, cemetery-dwelling, naked neighbor quite well—came out to see what all the commotion was about. What they found at the edge of the shore was more shocking than the dead pigs. This frightful man who had terrorized them was now "… sitting at the feet of Jesus, clothed and in his right mind …" (Luke 8:34 ESV).

Talk about a farfetched before-and-after image. From naked and in a state of madness to clothed and in his right mind. No longer being driven, darting in and out of deserts and tombs, but sitting quietly. Can this really happen to someone?

The Beauty and Complexity of Light

I say all this to prepare you for what happens next in my story, if you're still reading it after my telling of the mysterious hand appearing in the middle of my suicidal moment. I get it. There is little doubt that someone in my state of mind easily could have experienced hallucinations. Trust me, in many ways, it would be easier to just leave the "hand part" out of my narrative altogether. Certain reporters and other media outlets that have told my story have sometimes done just that. They say it's just a little "too kooky" for their audiences. It doesn't offend me; they have to consider the people to whom they write and broadcast. (It's even a little difficult to bring up with the Christian audiences I often speak to these days. There were no scars on the hand—so did it belong to Jesus, or an angel? I still don't know.)

But if you really want to know how someone like me gets from *that* point to *this* one, the hand is a critical detail. It was something that I didn't choose and honestly, something I *wouldn't* choose because, after all, it would be a lot easier to tell this crazy story without something quite so … well, crazy. But if conveniently leaving out the most easily dismissible detail also happens to omit the truest answer to the critical question regarding why I didn't die (and perhaps why many others didn't die as well) in that school office, then what's the point of not dying there in the first place?

So why didn't I die? Again, it all begins with the hand.

When my fingers finally touched the mysterious hand in front of me, everything instantly changed. It was as if one light switch—the one connected to deep, innermost destructive torment—was turned off, and another light switch—one bringing a sense of calm in a way I had never imagined even existed—was flipped on.

Boom.

Everything in that moment drastically changed. As the rest of my story will repeatedly reveal, this one moment didn't make me perfect, leave me without doubts, or purge me from major faults. I would go on to make many more mistakes in life, even lose my way at times. But in terms of my mental and emotional state—that is, the unseen, internal cage that was ensnaring me with violence, hopelessness, and torment—I was set free the moment I touched that hand.

My emotional rage completely subsided. There had been within me a furious storm, complete with hundred-foot waves, that suddenly transformed into a smooth sea of pristine glass. Violence gave way to calm, and darkness gave way to a new light I had never before experienced.

Now to be clear, I had absolutely no clue whose hand I had just touched. There was no voice. No name spoken out of thin air. No identity revealed. And quite honestly, no explanation regarding the strange encounter I had just lived through. I did not suddenly have all the answers; in fact, I suddenly had more of the questions. *What in the world am I doing here? Why have I been wishing death and destruction upon all these people? How could something so nefarious seem so right?*

It was as if I had suddenly come awake in the middle of a nightmare with a clearness that one simply cannot experience when trapped in the dreamy illusions of sleep. A light had inexplicably found me and began to brighten all the dark corners of reality around me. To my surprise, my initial emotional reaction was one of intense relief—the voices were gone. It was as if my mind suddenly had room to breathe, if that makes sense. This relief also produced in me a profound sense of gratitude, even though I didn't know whom to thank. My heart felt like it was actually beating again.

As clarity kept flooding in, the relief I was feeling also gave me room to feel the weight of the situation. I looked over at the hostages and suddenly I could again comprehend that they were just innocent people. I envisioned their families, who were worried sick about them. I saw their parents. Their children. Their futures.

I couldn't see the absolute mayhem that was occurring outside the school, but as any modern Google image search of the event will reveal, it was total chaos. At one point, terrified kids and teachers were running away from the building as fast as they could. Law enforcement officers met them and attempted to wrangle them to safety. Some events make "ripples." I had started a national tsunami.

What had I done?

In certain movies, there are scenes when all the lights go out and all you can hear is the sound of confused voices trying to find their way in the dark. It is a cinematic technique that allows the potential for whole stories to change in ways that surprise both the characters and the audience, especially when the lights come back on and a new villain, a new hero, or an unexpected variable has entered the room directly next to the characters. As soon as they see what has changed while they were in the dark, they are forced to react to the new context. It can be funny. It can be scary. Regardless, it changes everything.

When the "lights" came on for me, I could suddenly see the true situation in which I was standing. I was awakened to the very sober reality of the nightmare I had created. The light was incredible, but it also illuminated a lot of scary things. I stood there feeling like a completely different person but still wielding the same loaded gun I had carried under my coat into the school the day before. I was faced with the grave realization of who I now was: a school shooter who had taken nine hostages into captivity.

Such clarity of mind—the clarity I had wanted more than anything—also made it abundantly clear that this wasn't going to end well for me.

Again, earlier, I had cut off all communication with the Don Grant, the SWAT negotiator, but thankfully, I had been able to plug the phone back into the wall and reestablish contact. Don became my lifeline. While I know that his job was to calm me down and help manage all my heightened emotions, years later, something would become apparent that I had suspected from the beginning: Don's kindness to me was more than just doing his job.

I had moved from a state of unbridled rage to a state of extreme anxiety. Don's voice did something to help calm this part of me, at least enough to make a few better decisions before the end. It deeply impacted me that in the middle of such an inhumane situation—one I had created—another human was actually talking to me like I was also a human. To everyone else on the outside, I was a monster—and rightly so. I knew what Don was doing, but even so, I found a strange sense of comfort in his voice.

I will never forget something he told me that day over the phone. He said that if I were to get out of this alive and serve my time, then one day, we would go and have a beer together. I know that may not sound like much to most people, but his ability to create an image in my mind of a moment in the future that was actually positive—or even normal—was a fascination to me. The thought that I would ever be able to sit down in a restaurant across the table from a friend was a wonderful fantasy that I temporarily enjoyed indulging, but the truth was, I knew it was a pipe dream.

In my mind, there was no scenario that didn't include me leaving Lake Braddock High School in a body bag … but the thing was, I no longer wanted *anyone else* to leave the school that way.

I know it may be hard to believe, but I had become so struck with empathy for my captives that their wellbeing became much more important to me than my own. I do not say this to in any way paint myself as a hero or even as a sympathetic character in this story. No, I was a villain's villain. I only mean that something in my mind had seriously shifted from a desire to destroy innocent people to a desire to make sure no one was destroyed except the one who was so far from innocence: myself.

I wrestled with the fact that my hostages were innocent people who could still get hurt because it was very possible that this entire situation would escalate into scenarios that were out of my control. I deserved to be killed because of the cowardly choices I had made, but I had placed these people in a dangerous situation they did not deserve.

So Don and I began discussing a strategy in which I traded hostages for food and drinks. Two-by-two, I began releasing them to freedom, knowing that each exit was like a countdown to the ending I deserved. To me, there was a firing squad of twelve SWAT officers from the Fairfax County Police Department just waiting to engage me the moment I stepped one inch outside my little concrete fortress. They were armed with M16 assault rifles, which could shoot between seven hundred and 950 rounds per minute.

It would only take a round or two to do me in.

To be clear, I fully realized that although something— or someone—had given me the miraculous gift of some inner light, I was still about to experience physical death. Oddly enough, I was okay with it all. I deserved death and even longed for it, just no longer from the place of mental torment that had brought me to this destructive brink in the first place. Before, I had felt that death was the only way out of my torment … now, death felt like the only way to atone for my wrongs.

I found myself in a completely different kind of standoff, but no one on the outside knew about it. And even if they did, who would believe it? After all, *once a shooter* starts down the path I was on, there is no turning back, right? I had long since passed the point of no return.

Death meant something different to me now. I had wanted to die two nights before just to silence the voices of crippling despair within, but now, I actually felt the peace I had been seeking to find in death—and somehow it allowed me to be okay with dying. I knew that even in death, everything would be okay.

So for the next seven hours, as this impossible situation began to play out to its rightful end, I prepared for my rightful ending as well. I had walked alone through the front doors of a normal, unsuspecting high school in Burke, Virginia. And now, as I was about to leave that same school in a body bag that I deserved, there was a good chance no one would ever know that though I was *once a shooter*, in my now-peaceful heart, I was a shooter no more.

TRUST

At that point in my life, I did not trust the police—not in the least. Having spent most of my turbulent childhood in one of their homes, I had many of my own reasons for this distrust. So after I began negotiating the release of hostages for food and drinks, I remember feeling a sense of anxiety that one of the cops might accidentally shoot one of the innocent hostages, thinking they were me. This is just where my mind was at in that moment of my life.

As I began releasing them two at a time, I instructed the hostages to put their hands in the air so the police would immediately see they were unarmed and not the gunman. I knew that I was the target, not them, but at this point, there had somehow been no bloodshed—and I wanted it to stay that way until the end finally came for me. I calmly assured each of the remaining hostages that they would be fine—it must have been a strange thing to hear from a school shooter.

I released hostages every hour or so until finally, only one remained with me in the room: a teacher. I had already seen a mysterious hand that kept me from killing myself; I had no idea that I was about to experience yet another other-worldly display of compassion for someone who couldn't deserve it any less. We both seemed to know what I was really thinking: that she was the last person I would ever be around before the cops took me out for good.

In fact, that was my plan: suicide by cop. As soon as all of the hostages were out of harm's way, it would be very easy to provoke the police to do what none of them wanted to do. Did I really want to die? Yes—just not in the same way as before. I just knew I was in too deep. If I'm being real, I was thinking like a coward. I didn't want to have to face the consequences of my actions—the long path that lay ahead of me that, in my mind, consisted of nothing but a long, brutal existence in a dark, cold prison. Since I finally had some peace in my mind, it made more sense to skip all that future trouble and just let the police do their job.

The time finally arrived to release the last hostage, but to my surprise, she refused to go. I was dumbfounded. This lady had been stuck in that hell with me for the entire ordeal, almost twenty-one hours at that point. Freedom was finally available to her—the chance to rejoin her no doubt mortified family on the other side of this nightmare. But no matter what I said, she refused to leave. To this day, I don't know if she sensed that something had changed in me, or if she just had an intuition about what was about to happen.

"I'm not leaving," she said with deep concern in her voice. "They will kill you if I leave. You are just a confused kid and you haven't hurt anyone. I'm not going to leave you."

Truly, she was like an angel. She sought to protect me without regard for her own life. I have thought about that sweet lady more times than I can count over the past thirty-five years.

There was another significant variable contributing to my inability to think straight in these crucial moments: the injury to my hand that I had sustained when I busted out the glass with the butt of my rifle was still bleeding. After this many hours, I had lost quite a lot of blood, which rendered me extremely weak and woozy. The truth is, that precious teacher probably could have overtaken me had she chosen to try. Her goals for me were obviously different—she didn't just want the whole thing to be over (as I did); she also wanted me to live. I think that in my heart of hearts, somewhere down deep, I trusted her.

"This is as it should be," I said. "I deserve this, but you don't, so please just go because I don't want you to get hurt. Please!" My begging continued for about a half hour, but she wasn't going to budge. Once I realized I wasn't going to get rid of her, I began devising an alternate plan that would still cause the police to shoot me, but keep her from being hurt in the process. Again, I wasn't being a hero—I was being a coward.

"Okay, it's time," I said. "Walk with me, but slowly!" I don't think I realized quite how weak I had become because instead of walking together, she had to hold me up, practically carrying the right side of my body. We moved very slowly.

As we stumbled out the door of the office into the hallway, my rifle was still hanging from my left arm. The SWAT officers were waiting for our emergence, each with a bead on me, just waiting for my next move. I think every person in the hallway was holding his or her breath—this was the moment of truth.

Once we had inched closer to the center of the hall, the SWAT commander shouted at the teacher, "Get away from him *now*!" This was the moment that I knew was coming— my chance to end it all. I shoved her away from me with all the energy that I had left because that would ensure they could get a clear shot at me without hitting her. I was now completely exposed with no angel to protect me.

The SWAT commander continued slinging commands. "Now drop the gun!" I turned the barrel of my rifle away from the police in case there was a misfire and threw it across the hall. It landed on the floor about six feet away from me.

"Get down on the floor!"

I had complied with every one of his directives ... until now. I truly believed the police would certainly shoot me on the spot if I were to dive for the gun, so that's what I did. I dove for the ground and lunged for the rifle, my fingers just inches from touching it.

There was complete silence, except for a barrage of "clicking" noises as each of the SWAT officers disengaged the safety on his M16. I don't know how long I lay there reaching, only inches from my gun. It had to be mere seconds … the longest seconds of my life. The commander shouted, "Keep your hands away from the gun!"

Just then, it happened … again.

The mysterious hand reappeared.

In that moment, I once again felt that I was facing an epic choice: life or death. Life in the hand or death in the gun. I was so awestruck that it was happening again, and honestly just so tired of resisting, that I reached out and touched it yet again.

The next thing I knew, my hands were behind my back, and I was on the ground in police custody. They did what they had to do to apprehend me. It was not a gentle process.

The long nightmare for all the people I had terrorized was finally over. I had entered the school with the intent of wreaking havoc and mass destruction, and from an emotional and property standpoint, that mission was accomplished. But as I was being led out of Lake Braddock High School, everything in my life had changed—and in ways that I couldn't even begin to fathom.

There are no pigs in my story, but there was a demented young man living among the virtual tombstones—residing near death—and bringing destruction to the community around him. And yet somehow, no one had been destroyed, not even me. In a very unique way, I was clothed and in my right mind, sitting in the back of a police cruiser.

What should have been the last day of life somehow became the first day of a new life altogether, even though there was a long and winding road ahead of me.

CHAPTER 3

What (and Why) Now?

That was 1982.

   This is not.

Before I continue the details of what happened next in my story, I think it is probably wise to pause and remind you that the world we lived in back then was quite different from the world we live in today. In 1982, the horrors of Columbine were still seventeen years away. That's a long time.

For most people, Columbine felt like the event that changed the expectations of the world forever, mainly because what happened there to those innocent kids has happened to too many other innocent kids since then.

But in 1982, while what happened in Burke, Virginia, did make national headlines, it didn't seem to open the floodgates to more and more school shootings as regular, expected occurrences ... and thank God for this! The whole idea of school shootings was still foreign to most people, as it should be. After all, schools *should be* the safest places in our country because they are the places that contain that which (or better said, who) is most valuable to all of us. For 180 days every year, millions of kids pile into hundreds of thousands of buildings and classrooms all across the nation—and for the most part, almost all of them safely find their way out at the end of each of those 180 days.

But somewhere along the way, our collective expectations have been rocked by events that have forever transformed the way we feel about schools. I think this change is similar to the way September 11 changed our national consciousness and expectations about homeland security. There had certainly been terrorist attacks before that day, like the bombing of the federal building in Oklahoma City in 1995, and even the previous attempt on the World Trade Center in 1993. But those appalling events didn't seem to create a constant, collective anxiety in the American public regarding *when* (not if) the next terrorist attack would occur.

But all that seemed to change on September 11. Perhaps our perceptions changed because of the sheer vastness of the devastation and loss of life. Perhaps it occurred because of the seemingly unimaginable way the attacks themselves occurred. For our generation, the idea of airplanes and airports being some of the most unsafe places in our world was completely foreign. Obviously, I suppose that evil-minded terrorists could have done what was done on September 11 long before then, but since they didn't, our collective expectation never conceived it could happen.

Until it did.

After that, our cultural consciousness was forever changed. Kids began watching the skies, worried that any passing airplane might be hijacked and on its way to some unthinkable mission of destruction. In this new world, every time we go to the airport to fly anywhere, even with our children for a family vacation, we expect a process that includes us being thoroughly scanned, searched, and possibly even detained if something in our carry-on bag sends up a red flag. The world changed after 9-11, and so did our daily lives.

But kids in my generation never had to worry in these ways because such things simply were not in our conscious or subconscious list of things to be concerned about.

Just as 9-11 forever changed our perceptions of air travel and terrorism, Columbine seemed to be the moment that the national consciousness about the danger of school shootings changed forever. Parents and kids alike now had something very real to be afraid of in the very places they had always assumed were the safest.

When each one of these tragedies flashed across the screen over the years that followed my own crazy moment of mass stupidity, my heart broke in ways I doubt most people can understand. After all, most people have never walked into a school with a rifle and the malicious intent to kill as many people as possible. I'm a member of a pretty shameful club, but it does offer me a unique glimpse into the tragedies that now seem to be commonplace in our culture.

This brings me to a key question you no doubt have: why am I sharing this story now? Well, the truth is, I just feel like

I am supposed to. To be quite honest, it would be easier not to. For thirty-six years, I have been running from this story. For thirty-six years, I have lived ashamed of who I was and what I did. I have lived in the shadows, trying to fly under the radar.

I have changed my name multiple times, trying to outrun that stupid kid who entered that school in 1982. He didn't kill anyone, but in some ways, I have lived much of my life running from him, as if he is constantly pointing his loaded rifle my direction. It has felt as if it's just a matter of time before he finally takes me out for good.

Along my journey, which will unfold in the pages to come, I have lived in many different cities and experienced many horrible—and also incredible—things. I have made a ton of mistakes, although none of them have ever had the severe earthly, tangible consequences of the one I made when I was eighteen years old. I have been married. I have divorced. I have two children, one of whom became a US Marine. At the time of this writing, I have five beautiful grandchildren. And every time I look into their eyes, I know that I don't deserve them—or any of the grace and beauty that has been extended to me.

You see, I could just lay low. Keep to myself. Live as I lived for so long—as just another guy with whom you do business every day, go to church with every week, and run into at the grocery store occasionally. No one would ever have to know.

But this brings me back to Columbine and the more than two hundred school shootings that have followed over the last two decades. Every time I have witnessed these atrocities flash across my television screen, an almost unbearable pressure has overtaken me—the feeling that I'm still just that coward who tried to end his life back in 1982. Kids are dying and kids are killing, and no one seems to have any answers, right? And yet here I sit as one of the few people in this world who has actually experienced the darkness that overtakes a person's mind in such moments. And I'm basically hiding out in my new life ... not a perfect life, but definitely far from the prison or cemetery that I deserve.

Of course, I am not implying that because I was a school shooter, I have some perfect insight into the minds of every other school shooter in this world. I am sure each of them has unique family backgrounds, reasoning (or lack thereof), and mental health situations.

I'm not trying to speak *for* them ... I'm actually trying to speak *to* them. I may not share their exact situation, but I do share their experience.

Columbine. Virginia Tech. Northern Illinois University. Sandy Hook. And too many others. Each one of these has reminded me not only of what I *did*, but also of what I *haven't been doing*—that is, sharing my story. And yes, I know this story will not reach everyone, but if my willingness to share it at live events, in the media, and in this book helps even one potential school shooter avoid the path of destruction before him, then honestly, it will be worth it. No, this may not be a bestseller, but I don't think there is an amount of money that can be ascribed to the saving of lives.

I should know ... because my life was spared.

The school shooting in Parkland, Florida, was the one that finally pushed me out of the shadows for good. The vicious spree of bullets at Marjory Stoneman Douglas High

School on Valentine's Day, 2018, was the worst high school mass shooting in American history. That day, seventeen students were senselessly gunned down, with seventeen others sustaining injuries from the attack. For me, that was the last straw. I had to speak up.

Much of my story to come will explain my mindset in the years that followed my own rampage at Lake Braddock High, so I don't want to get ahead of myself. I do, however, want you to at least understand the timing of why I am speaking up *now*. The rest of the story will unfold, revealing the ins and outs of my journey, but as I sat there watching those kids run from yet another school building, I realized that people's lives are literally being lost and no one knows what to do about it.

All of the conversations are about school security, gun control, political activism, governmental oversight, mental health, and a host of other issues. And believe you me, I think each of these plays an important role in the conversation and we must be good stewards in addressing each one with diligence, compassion, and common sense. However, I can't help but feel that same unbearable weight that every parent, family member, and expert on the news is carrying: the absolute confusion of it all. There are many facets to this issue, but no one seems to know how to stop it … and they know they don't know.

The general American feeling about school shootings seems to be a combination of helplessness and hopelessness. The helplessness is caused by what I just mentioned: there is no real sense of what would actually stop this horrific trend from continuing. Parents are generally wired with the innate desire to use precaution and take action in the daily process of helping their kids move toward maturity. The underlying and most fundamental element of the parental instinct (though it certainly varies from person to person) is to keep their kids safe. They lock the doors at night. Many arm themselves with all kinds of weapons that they could access if they ever needed to in an emergency. They install monitored personal security systems to alert them if an intruder ever breaches their homes' perimeters. And when they have to leave the house, they make sure their kids are riding in vehicles equipped with the latest technology that ensures the safest ride and the best possible features in the event of a crash. They also install filters on their phones and computers, as well as any other safety precaution we can find to keep them safe from predators online, and prevent exposure to content they have no business knowing at a young age—and in some cases, at any age.

But when it comes to dropping our kids off at school or the bus stop, a parent's proactive power of precaution is thwarted—or at least that's how it can feel. While we don't want to live in an unreasonable state of fear and anxiety (after all, we can't always be everywhere and prevent every bad thing in this world from happening), it seems we should at least be able to send our innocent children into a school building without the fear that someone might gun them down. Sure, we can't stop tornadoes, earthquakes, or even an outbreak of measles, but it feels like we should be able to stop these shootings ... and the fact that we can't creates an overwhelming sense of helplessness.

This helplessness lends itself to hopelessness. Hope is the key ingredient to life. Hope is more than a feeling; it is tied to belief and, regardless of your religious or irreligious leanings, to a sense of faith. We have confined faith to some mystical, confession-based realm where people try to speak their desired reality into existence, and some even claim that God Himself will do just such a thing for them if they just "have enough faith." This kind of faith strays far from a realistic and basic understanding of the concept itself: faith is believing and hoping in something that you can't see or hasn't yet happened. Scripture even supports this definition, tethering faith to hope in an unbreakable bond.[1]

Religious thought aside, we all have a level of faith in something. Even the ones who think themselves to be chronic doubters, conspiracy theorists, or otherwise incapable of believing in something unseen still exercise the basic principles of faith on a daily basis. The act of simply sitting down in a chair without first getting down on our hands and knees to thoroughly inspect and determine if it has the strength and structural integrity to bear our weight, is, in a small way, exercising faith in the chair—a belief that it will be able to hold us up, coupled with the hope that it will do so, which leads us to take the action of sitting.

While I know this example may be elementary, it proves that we all have faith in something. That is the essence of faith.

Hopelessness, therefore, has occurred when the "chair" we have always had faith would hold us up—in this case, our children's safety at school—has disintegrated beneath us. The hopelessness is compounded by the sense that things weren't always this way and that they certainly shouldn't be this way. It's one thing to slip while chopping vegetables with a sharp knife and cut yourself—you are aware of the possibility that using a blade at all can hurt you. But what has happened in our school systems is like finding out that the vegetables themselves might spontaneously explode in your hands: it has rocked our sense of what should be, as if the rules of the universe themselves have been turned upside down.

Watching innocent elementary children being needlessly butchered by deranged gunmen hits us in this bedrock area of our hearts, robbing us of a general sense of hope that was once based upon what we could expect: the simple essence of right and wrong. Emotionally, it leaves us not really knowing which way is up. We have lost our confidence, and for good reason.

Here's the deal: I don't know all of the answers either, but I do think there are other questions we can be asking. I know that I once walked a mile in the shoes of a school shooter. It is a situation in which all hope seems to be lost, and yet here I stand in a new life far removed from that old one. I'm not the smartest, most educated, or even most articulate guy on all the topics related to this hellish subject, but I have been to hell and back.

More than just firsthand knowledge, I have a verified, eyewitness account about the very hope that everyone concerned about this issue is grasping for. I had a front-row seat to the freak show … or I guess you could say I was the one in the center ring, just waiting to be trampled underfoot by the elephants. And yet somehow, I did not just survive, but have been completely redeemed from all that should have destroyed me. How can I keep silent when others are crying out for help?

I know I may be the last person in this world that some people would want to hear from on this issue, but I feel compelled to join the right side of this fight. I no longer want to sit back comfortably in my living room while more innocent kids lose their lives on national television. I may be the last person you *want* to hear from, but I very well may be one of the first ones you *need* to hear from, if for no other reason than I have been where most people have only dreamt about in their worst nightmares.

I know it probably sounds shallow, but stepping back into the spotlight of this particular discussion opens me up to a lot of fair ridicule that would be easier to just avoid. In fact, it also puts my livelihood at risk. I am a business owner now, and for years, none of my clients have had any idea about my past. It has been nice to just be good old TJ Stevens, the guy who shows up on time and does a decent job setting up and providing ongoing support for your company's network issues.

Before I started working with producers and writers who have helped me tell my story in all these various ways, I had some very difficult phone calls to make, mainly to clients. I had to let them know they were about to see my story on national television or in bookstores—and it was a story they knew nothing about. There was a chance they wouldn't want to work with me anymore, so I wanted to respect them enough to let them hear it from me first.

To be clear, I know this is a selfish line of thought, and I'm aware that you're probably thinking that in light of what I chose to do, I don't deserve to have a business, much less my freedom. You may be thinking that it seems fairly petty and shortsighted of me to worry about these kinds of things when I was one of the criminals in question—the ones who are dragging our nation through this ordeal.

If you think this of me, your point is well taken … I actually agree with you. Nothing about the mercy that has been shown to me has been *fair*. I don't deserve a family, children, grandchildren, or a successful business. I certainly never thought I would have these things, but the fact is, I do—and throughout the pages to come, I'd like to tell you how all this grace came my way.

When The "Supernatural" Doesn't Seem So Super

Yes, I know my "hand" story is extreme. I can't deny this … and I don't want to. I understand the reticence to talk about such things in today's culture. We are inundated with so much information from so many, often conflicting, sources that it is hard to know who or what to believe, especially considering the way supernatural things are framed in our society. For the most part, the supernatural is seen as either religious fanaticism or as mystical paranormal activity. It is either about the *rantings* of some crazy preacher detached from reality or the *ratings* of some crazy television show also detached from reality (though sometimes ironically labeled "reality" television).

I understand the tension, but I wonder if there isn't a supernatural reality not confined to either of these. In other words, maybe the extreme expressions of the supernatural are distracting us from looking at the variable itself—almost as if an unusual, long-lasting, intermittently occurring sequence of chronic flooding and chronic drought were to somehow cause us to begin questioning the validity of rain itself.

Watching video footage of Nikolas Cruz, the nineteen-year-old expelled student who viciously murdered all those kids in Parkland, I am reminded of so many eerily familiar things. He sits in a prison cell, shackled to the floor, punching himself in the face and putting an imaginary gun to his head over and over again as he rocks back and forth, conversing in agony with the voices in his head. It is obvious that he is hopelessly lost in a darkness so deep that it's hard to even acknowledge its existence—to do so is simply too disturbing for most people. We find what little comfort we can solely in the fact that he is locked up somewhere far, far away from our children.

But we know that such comfort is a merely a false sense of security because, while this particular young man will never again be allowed to terrorize another school, we know he is not the only one out there. The next shooter could be sitting in his own bedroom as we speak, wrestling with the tormenting voices in his own head, cradling a gun and contemplating the next fatal incident for the next news cycle.

As a nation, we are all experiencing the fruits of this deep darkness. When something unspeakable happens, we watch in horror as it is replayed over and over again on the news. For some, it hits home in their own schools and families. But even if we don't personally know a victim, it still hits home for all of us. The level of loss and devastation is mind-boggling, and again, we feel helpless to do anything. There are so many components involved, and we must acknowledge them all. Mental health. Bullying. Abuse. Trauma. And yes, even social media.

After all, before the Parkland shootings, Nikolas Cruz posted a video where he let the world know, in no uncertain terms, what he was about to do. "My name is Nick, and I'm going to be our next school shooter of 2018. My goal is at least twenty people with an AR-15 and a couple of trace rounds. I think I can get it done. Location is Stoney Douglas, Parkland, Florida. It's going to be a big event. When you see me on the news, you'll know who I am. [Laughing to himself.] You're all going to die."

What drives a young man to such a state of mind? None of us fully know—but I can tell you there is another component that can at least contribute to this situation: the spiritual.

Before I move on, it is probably helpful to distinguish between the terms "supernatural" and "spiritual." While they are certainly related, they are not necessarily one and the same. Why point out the difference? Because if we always think of anything that is spiritual as also being supernatural, we miss the fact that the spiritual is part of our daily lives, regardless of our awareness of it or lack thereof.

I am not necessarily speaking of "spiritual" in terms of faith or religion. I simply mean that our thoughts, wishes, values, and wills—all things that cannot be touched, seen, or dissected in a lab under a microscope—are the most real parts of our lives. And while our physiology and chemistry contributes to these things, none of them can be completely summed up in the study of synapses, nature, or nurture.

As one wise person put it, "'Spiritual' is not just something we *ought* to be. It is something we *are* and cannot escape, regardless of how we may think or feel about it. It is our nature and our destiny."[2]

I understand our hesitancy since so many quasi-teachers and religious fanatics on television seem to make a show out of exorcisms, have unnecessarily dramatic conversations with demons, and draw attention to countless other practices of that nature. This mixes the spiritual with the supernatural in ways that make the kind of discussion I want to have here difficult in "normal," everyday life. For that matter, so many of our movies focus on this area; filmmakers pride themselves upon their ability to create an exhilarating sense of fear or suspense in the viewer. Since we are just watching on a screen, we find it "fun" to be scared half to death by supernatural, gory thrillers. The result is that the spiritual either gets lumped in with strict religion or it becomes culturally confined to the realm of fantasy or entertainment.

And so we now live in a world that brushes off any reference to the spiritual as if it cannot be even a factor in the bigger picture of our daily lives—and the bigger picture of the epidemic of school shootings. Most of the experts, pundits, and government leaders have become afraid—perhaps rightfully so, considering how much the supernatural has been sensationalized and twisted to unhealthy ends—to even nominally admit the possibility of anything supernatural having a role in these tragic events. It is rarely acknowledged in any serious way.

Even so, most leaders are not afraid to ask the public to "keep the victims in your prayers."

My "What Now?"

If you had asked me about the "spiritual" when I was eighteen years old with a gun in my hand and hate in my heart, I don't think I would have had any answer whatsoever. It wouldn't have occurred to me. It was as if I was driving in fog at night down a dark road with the music up so loud I couldn't hear anything. I was only able to see the next few feet in front of me, and I had no idea that the bridge ahead of me was out.

Even if people on the side of the road had been screaming at me, warning me that painful destruction lay just ahead of me, I wouldn't have been able to hear them. It was just too dark. Too foggy. Too loud. And I was moving too fast.

That's just how life works, isn't it? Often, the path we are currently walking becomes the hardest to subjectively evaluate. A relationship seems so right in the beginning, but just ahead is infidelity or worse. A job opportunity seems perfect, but just ahead is stress, burnout, and office strife. A community seems to be the perfect place to connect and raise a family, but just ahead is trouble no one could see coming. As they say, sometimes you can be "too close" to something to see it for what it really is.

I can't speak for Nikolas Cruz or any of the other school shooters out there, but I can speak as one who drove off the bridge in the middle of the fog and lived to tell about it—and what I know is that I was completely unaware of what was happening to me while it was happening. I was too close. Too lost in the fog of my own past pain to slow down long enough to see or hear the warning signs. I raced ahead, right past all the logical, ever-present reasons not to do such a thing.

What will keep the next school shooter from the doing the same thing? If I couldn't see it, what will make him see it? Again, I'm not the answer guy, but I know I never began to experience real hope until something reached me *inside* the car, not from *outside*. No matter how thick the fog may be, how loud the music may be, or how fast you may be driving, when someone is sitting next to you, they have the best chance of making you able to hear.

For me, this is what the spiritual really is. There were teachers in that school who were begging me not to hurt myself or others, but I couldn't really hear them. Don Grant did his very best to reason with me—to help me see that I was driving myself off a bridge and into certain death. I mean, who does that? Who wants to destroy themselves? Instinctively, no one. But when we are in motion within the fog, we seem to lose our instincts and just floor it toward whatever seems right in our own heads.

Nothing reached me until someone got into my head with me. I didn't ask them to do so—and I certainly didn't slow down to give them time to open the door. No, it was something spiritual … something more than just what I could see, hear, or touch. And yet, it was the most real thing that has ever happened to me—the reason I didn't follow through on everything the other voices in my head were begging me to do. Yes, I was responsible for every bit of it—I'm just saying that I wasn't alone in it all.

I think we can acknowledge the spiritual component of every human being and still hold them responsible for their choices. The idea that we have to pick between the two—

between the influence of the spiritual and the accountability required for physical actions—reflects the extreme culture we live in today. Just scroll through Twitter or Facebook for a few minutes and see how many moderate, mild opinions you find regarding politics, religion, or even relationships. For the most part, ours is a culture in which each person's opinion is king and anyone who says otherwise is immediately convicted as a bona fide idiot, with no due process. There are few real discussions across a table, where reasonable conversations can occur between reasonable people.

I hope you will not convict me in your mind for either acknowledging the spiritual or not acknowledging it enough or in the exact words your particular viewpoint prefers. I hope you will simply hear from my story the fact that what happened to me was more than just mental, physical, or emotional (though each of those components were certainly present and had some effect).

The spiritual part of my life was so real and so broken that I didn't even realize it had set me on fire, but when someone interacted with this part of me, the flames immediately subsided. The spiritual was the place where everything changed for me. That may not be popular to say, but I gave up the idea of being popular a long time ago.

There was another guy who went on a killing rampage. His name was Saul, and he was completely convinced that hurting innocent men, women, and children—just because they had a different religion than him—was absolutely the right thing to do. He literally considered what was most wrong to be most right. He was upside down. I can relate.

But in the middle of one of his "mission trips" to round up more innocent people, he had his own "hand" experience. It happened on a road leading into a city called Damascus. A great light knocked him to the ground and blinded him. A voice spoke to him from that light—the voice of the very One whose followers Saul was seeking to destroy.

This "spiritual" encounter changed everything for Saul, eventually even his name (I've had a few name changes in my time, so I understand the significance). The craziest part, however, is that the Light that should have destroyed him for his many crimes instead invited him to join the very cause he was tearing down. The Voice reasoned with him that the path he was on was actually harming him. In other words, the peace he was seeking could not be found on the path he was walking.

Some translations include a poignant observation by the Voice: "It is hard for thee to kick against the pricks" (Acts 26:14 KJV). This expression was a common Greek proverb at the time, something that an educated Jewish man like Saul definitely would have recognized. In the original language, "pricks" referred to sticks used to steer oxen in the right direction out in the fields. A prick had at its tip a pointed piece of iron. Obviously, when the animal resisted the direction of the one steering it, the result would be the prick, or goad, causing more pain instead of less.

I'm not a scholar or a historian, but I wonder if anyone else had ever tried to talk Saul out of his destructive ways. Reason with him. Get through to him about all the ways his current actions were not just hurting others, but also himself. Who knows? What we do know is that whatever was causing him to go down the path didn't change until he was reached on a spiritual level. Obviously, I'm not saying that we shouldn't listen, speak reasonably, educate, encourage people to go to counseling, seek medical help, or the like. All of these are very important. I'm only saying there are times when, in addition to all of those other things, we should also be willing to admit the need for spiritual help as well.

The moment that hand reached out for me was definitely my "road to Damascus" moment. It was the first time that the most critical, wounded part of me—the spiritual part—was met with a spiritual response. It was a once-in-a-lifetime moment; even so, it was most definitely a beginning, not an ending. I did not arrive at a place of instantaneous health and maturity, even though I was instantly relieved from the onslaught of the violent voices in my head. A great light had found me, but there was much more work for that light to do in my heart for years to come.

Saul's experience was the same. After the Light knocked him down and the Voice spoke to him, he found himself unable to see. What a change! Saul had been transformed from a powerful, violent crusader to a confused, humbled, blind man. He had to reach out and ask for the help of others. He also had much to learn about the Voice that had spoken to him … and his journey of discovering and growing in that knowledge lasted for years to come.

As I was placed in the back of that police car, I also still had a lot to discover and learn about the hand that had rescued me. I was also going to need help from others to figure it out—a lot of help.

Unlike Saul, I did not even know the name of my Rescuer yet.

CHAPTER 4

Freedom Lost
... Freedom Found

Being led away from the school in handcuffs was the first time since the whole ordeal had started that I was actually able to personally witness the crazy scene I had created outside the school. I remember seeing literally hundreds of police and law enforcement officers, helicopters, and vehicles scattered everywhere. Members of the media also gathered by the dozens beside their huge collections of cameras and lights.

Our first stop was the local hospital to tend to the wound on my hand. As soon as I'd been treated, it was another ride to the Fairfax County Detention Center, where I was placed in a holding cell, alone. When I arrived at the detention center, I saw hundreds of media already gathered there as well.

Soon I was taken to an interrogation room. The investigators who were about to interrogate me were in the interesting situation of already knowing beyond a shadow of a doubt that I had done the deed for which I had been arrested. The prolonged hostage situation had placed me in a situation in which I literally had no grounds for negotiation. I was guilty—they knew it, and I knew it, but they had to do due diligence to make sure I had due process.

But as they began compiling all the statements, data, and evidence that would eventually be presented before a judge at my trial, there was something they just couldn't figure out. One of them asked me directly, "So, how did you know?"

"Know what?" I replied in confusion.

"How did you know when the green light was given to shoot to kill?"

Apparently, the green light had been given to take me out and end the threat to the innocent hostages several times during the ordeal. In those moments, however, I somehow never gave the snipers a clean shot. I would always be conveniently positioned behind a person or thing that would keep them from pulling the trigger. But when the red light was given—that is, the command to "hold fire," I apparently consistently showed myself to be an easy target. They wanted to know if somebody on the outside was somehow feeding me information. Who was working with me? Who was protecting me? I looked at them in disbelief. I dropped my head on the cold interrogation table and just wept. I just couldn't fathom why I had been spared.

Sometimes, I still can't.

My family sacrificed quite a lot to get me the best possible legal representation possible. In fact, my attorney later served as Attorney General for the Commonwealth of Virginia. But at that moment, I had very little comfort and hope for the future. My crimes were quite severe.

Early in our talks, my attorney informed me that I could be facing up to 144 years in prison on account of many felony charges against me. That number stuck with me. From that moment forward, I truly believed any hope of freedom was gone forever.

Oddly enough, the moment of the first physical contact with the police officers at the school was itself a moment of freedom, even though they had me on the ground with a knee in my back as they searched me for more weapons. It was a relief of sorts, mainly because the death I had sought was now in my rearview mirror. I had played chicken with death and somehow managed to dodge it.

But that momentary feeling of relief quickly faded as I continued to process in real time what I had done and what kind of life now lay ahead of me. I was only eighteen years old, but I knew I would spend the rest of my life in prison. It is hard enough to be a young adult looking out at the great big scary life ahead of you with all of the decisions to be made, relationships to develop, and experiences to be had. But for me, everything ahead was now tinted ... tainted by my own cowardly, absurd actions.

I felt the weight of prison. I knew I was going to have to fight to survive—to establish and preserve my safety. My sanity. My manhood. I knew that my physical body would now be confined for eternity—from a prison cell in the years to come to a casket somewhere in the distant future. I had blown it, and the more I thought about it, the more I once again longed for death.

I remember telling my attorney that I wanted to be executed.

As I said, I was far from healthy or rehabilitated. I was still crying out for help, even though I didn't want anyone's help. I had first wanted to die to end the torment and pain in my head, but now, I wanted to die because I deserved it. I felt that I was filth, not even worthy to be in a prison cell. To incarcerate me would be a waste of taxpayers' money. I just wished someone would take my life.

The shame was almost unbearable. When I was in my dark place before, I didn't care what anyone thought, but that had all changed. I felt intense disgrace just thinking of how disappointed my family must have been now that they all knew what I had become. I knew the world wanted me dead, so the answer was simple …

Just give them what they want.

UNUSUAL SUSPECTS

After the police had fully processed me, I was sent to Central State Hospital in Petersburg for psychological evaluations. Back in the late nineteenth century, that facility had been known as the Central Lunatic Asylum. Though the name had been modernized, I certainly felt like a lunatic. I was supposed to stay there for up to thirty days until a determination could be made about my state of mind—and thus my ability to stand trial and sentencing.

My time in that facility was terrifying. They put me in a big, round room with a bunch of other patients. It was like living in a horror movie or hanging out with actors from *The Walking Dead* ... except they weren't acting. Some of them had really eaten people before. I didn't talk to anybody and tried to keep what wits I had left about me. The staffers tried to feed me certain meds, which I simply pocketed in my cheek and spit out after they walked away.

There were televisions in the hospital, so everyone around me knew what I had done and why I was there—so besides just being fresh meat, I was kind of a novelty to them, even though the last thing I wanted at that point was any extra attention. I had to sleep in a room with quite a few other patients. Some of them would walk up to me in the middle of the night and threaten to kill me, which I believed they would at a moment's notice. And while I was not opposed to dying and being done with the hopeless life ahead of me, that was not the way I wanted to go.

I was only there for six or seven days, but it was a terrifying experience. Thankfully, there was a big African American guy who took a liking to me. He called me "Horse" because I had a lot of hair and I was fairly stout. As far as I was concerned, he could have called me "Bear," "Kitten," or any other kind of animal in the forest—I was just glad that when he was near me, no one seemed willing to try to hurt me. There was no doubt in my mind that he protected me from being killed.

Like I said, it only took about six or seven days for the doctors to determine that there was nothing wrong with me that could keep me from standing trial and answering for my crimes. Thus my stay at Central State Hospital ended, and I was shipped back to the Fairfax County Detention Center ... back to lockup.

I spent the next six or seven months there, awaiting and undergoing my trial. That was when I began learning how to survive in prison. I was a loner and wanted to stay that way, but for the most part, this didn't work out in jail. It was a communal experience—that is, there were groups and gangs everywhere, and your connection to people was the key to what happened to you. I refused to join a gang—it just wasn't for me. I was isolated and exposed like a sitting duck. I was in trouble, and I knew it.

I devised a plan that I hoped would make a huge statement, one that would last as long as I was stuck in lockup. Lucas was a huge African American with short hair and biceps bigger than my head. He had been convicted of murder. He was the most feared man in the detention center. One day during chow time, I walked up to him and just started sucker punching him over and over again as hard as I could.

I knew I was going to get beat up really bad, but I also knew that if I went after Lucas, everyone else might back off and leave me alone. The bottom line was that if I was crazy enough to jump him, everyone would assume that I was definitely crazy enough to jump them too. I just kept throwing punches like a madman, beating him across the entire mess hall. It was a good thing that I took him by surprise because it seemed to stun him so that I was able to keep getting punches in while everyone looked on.

Lucas finally came to himself enough to mount a defense, but luckily for me, the guards had reached us by then and had started *breaking us up* before he had the chance to *break my face*. My plan may have been rash, but it worked. I walked away from the brawl with a few bruises, but more importantly, with the reputation of being someone no one wanted to mess with. People still sometimes messed with me for sure, but at least for the time I had left in the detention center, I avoided the worst of it.

Oddly enough, Lucas and I actually went on to become very good friends. Prison life is strange that way. Respect is the name of the game, and respect within prison walls generally has to be earned at great cost. Even crazier than our friendship was the fact that our mothers also became friends during that time. I suppose it makes sense that two mothers might find their *way* to friendship while they are both regularly visiting their *wayward* sons. After I was transferred from the detention center to prison, I lost touch with Lucas, but I often wonder what became of him.

That Guy

At that point, I still felt lost—a lot like a blinded Saul. I was just stumbling forward, feeling my way along with the help of anyone I could find. Lucas was just one of the many people placed in my path for a particular moment or season who helped me in ways no one else could at the time. The teacher in the office who refused to leave me. The officers who could have pulled their triggers when I lunged for my rifle. The guy in the psych hospital who watched over me because I reminded him of a horse. Lucas.

There was also a local pastor named John Bonds who would sit with me and pray for me. John will resurface in my story down the road, but during this time, it was a big deal that he was just willing to visit a worthless felon, which is all I believed myself to be.

There would be many, many more people to come—and many of them were not the usual suspects you would expect to come to the aid of a soon-to-be-convicted school shooter. I wasn't asking for any of this help. It was more like I kept stumbling and people kept coming along to pick me up off the floor so I could find my next step. I was messed up, but it was still as if whatever had saved me from taking my own life in that school office was somehow saving me still, which included saving me from myself.

I was not a religious man at the time. I only knew that something spiritual had happened to me at the school, but I wasn't yet ready to fully commit to the idea of it having anything to do with faith or God. My level of self-worth was next to nothing, probably resulting from a combination of my own unique makeup and the extreme experiences from my childhood that had robbed me of feeling like anything but a complete failure. I thought of death often, as I had done for years.

But since I had nothing but time while I awaited my trial, I began to attend a little Bible study in the Fairfax County Detention Center. It was led by a pastor, but I don't remember his name or anything about his ministry. The meeting was obviously a voluntary thing, and most of the inmates who attended would never speak. We just listened.

I honestly do not remember any specific verses shared in those meetings, but I'm not sure the exact words were really the point. Just going was a huge deal for me. Even though I can't recall much, I do recall hearing that I was loved by God—so much so that He had sent a Savior, His only Son, to take the punishment I deserved. For a man sitting in jail, this concept was much more than just a "Sunday School" lesson that sounds good on paper, but doesn't have much application when you walk out the door back into the real world.

For me, there was no hope that I would ever walk out any door into any "real world." My world was now, and forever would be, confined to a life behind concrete walls and iron bars. I was facing the literal judgment of a literal judge who sat on a real bench with a real gavel. I was afraid of him, even though I knew I fully deserved whatever sentence he would hand down. I knew that in order for justice to be served, I had to be severely punished. I didn't want the punishment, but I agreed that it was right.

I think the concept of God as Judge is lost on many people in America today simply because most people rarely have to stand before a real judge for anything other than a speeding ticket that leads to driving school or perhaps a fine. And for most of them, there is a sense that, even if they were caught speeding, the judge is somehow unfair in passing down even menial sentencing. After all, everyone else is speeding too. Nobody's perfect, right? I mean, it's not like most of us are murderers, felons, or thieves—so as long we don't commit any of these major offenses, then we should be let off the hook.

That is the idea of "judge" that I think most people subconsciously apply to God. He seems harsh towards people who don't deserve it because most of us aren't really *that* bad. When it comes to our earthly justice system, this idea has some merit. The problem arises when we try to blanket the spiritual reality with earthly ideas, because the "I'm not that bad" defense before God not only doesn't hold water, it is not even the question He is asking.

At that point, even though I was still very far away from living as a man of faith, I had lost all desire to defend myself before any kind of judge—earthly or heavenly. I knew what was inside me, and I knew that it deserved steep judgment. I know that sounds strange, but I think this complete state of rock bottom in terms of mounting a common, human self-defense of my actions or intentions actually put me in a better position to hear the real message of the Gospel. I had neither the desire nor the energy to hold onto a single iota of self-righteousness.

I hadn't killed anyone, but that was merely a technicality—another feature of a completely mysterious grace that had protected me and others from the true darkness of myself. I was a killer at heart, and I knew it. My heart had been fully revealed not just to the whole world, but more importantly, to me. In terms of proclaiming myself "not that bad," the general, practical theology that most people seem to live by today, I had no leg to stand on.

Because of this complete belief in my unworthiness, the idea of the love of God was nothing less than completely revolutionary—and honestly, just too good to be true. Many people in our culture may be familiar with the song *"Amazing Grace,"* but because they consider themselves to be doing pretty well on their own merits, it is mostly just a song. Grace isn't so amazing when people don't think they really need it that badly.

Even though I knew nothing, I knew better than this for myself. The idea of any kind of grace, much less the kind that would stand in my place and pay the debt I fully owed, was truly amazing. So much so that I just couldn't believe it. Not yet.

Ironically, I think that many people—even those who go to church every week and check the box "Christian" on whatever form they may be filling out—don't actually believe grace is really *that* amazing. It is all too easy to fall into the mindset that the Gospel is really a technical message that gets us into Heaven sometime in a distant future we call eternity. We can feel pretty ambivalent toward a God who insists on judging us more harshly than we deserve, especially if we aren't as bad as *that* guy over there—the murderer, kidnapper, or robber. Again, no one's perfect, but at least I'm not as bad as *that* guy.

Except I *was that* guy.

My issue wasn't that I was shrugging off the grace of God as something other people needed more than I did. My issue was that I thought myself too bad to be able to accept it. Even so, the idea of it was planted in my troubled heart—and the seed wasn't just buried and forgotten. It may have been unseen for a long time, but it was there, sprouting, spreading, and ultimately growing in unseen places within me. I was far from seeing anything break through to the surface of my life, but a truly amazing grace was busy about an unexpected work within me in ways I couldn't even begin to fathom or verbalize.

CHAPTER 5

The Darkness before the Light

As I said before, my attorney originally told me I was facing up to 144 years in prison. At my age and in my state of mind, I never heard the "up to" part. I felt so guilty about what I had done that in my mind, the full sentence might as well have already been passed down. I was my own judge and executioner. But at my arraignment, the amount of time I was facing was changed to up to thirty-six years. Still, it brought me little comfort—that still seemed like a lifetime I couldn't process emotionally.

Regardless, the trial commenced, and the judge began to listen to all the testimony presented by both sides. As far as I was concerned, the prosecutor in my case had the easiest job in the history of jobs. The questions before the court weren't really regarding whether or not I had committed multiple heinous crimes but about what had caused me to enter such a state of mind and how severely I should be punished for it.

There was a lot about my past that needed to be shared with the courtroom—and it needs to be shared in this book as well. Even though it was shared back then, I haven't shared it since … and it wasn't made public at the time, for myriad reasons.

Up to now, I've presented to you a few of my thoughts about our need to at least recognize and address the spiritual components of the problems we keep facing in these school-shooting incidents. Now, I would like to show you how the physical, relational, and emotional parts of my own life affected me mentally and spiritually. This is still not easy for me to share, but again, my mission here is to speak truth in a way that might bring hope to someone out there who has either experienced loss or is contemplating inflicting great harm on others.

You see, I didn't just wake up one day and decide to hurt others and myself. I had actually been suicidal multiple times before, even though I was so young. There was a steady stream of pain and abuse that I had been running from for most of my life.

BDD

I have started to think of my life as a narrative divided into two distinct parts: before Doomsday, or BDD, and after

Doomsday, or ADD. Doomsday, in this case, was obviously the day I took hostages in my school.

When something tragic happens in our society, news reporters often interview the assailant's neighbors, trying to determine if what has occurred seems to be out of character or unexpected. Most times, neighbors reveal that the person usually kept to himself—and in some cases, that the incident seemingly "came out of nowhere" because the person in question was always so kind and "normal."

This speaks to the assumptions we all have about people. We generally assume that if we're not seeing or hearing negative things, then everything must be okay. I think this is part of our collective coping mechanism—we have a default need to think that everything is positive. Otherwise, we would have to live in a state of constant paranoia and fear, always wondering who is quiet on the outside but about to explode because of things happening on the inside.

My point here is not to cause us to always assume the negative; it is simply to point out that rarely does something just come "out of nowhere." Whatever happens in life usually *comes out of somewhere* very specific and distinct. When an earthquake hits, we tend at first only to see the vast damage done to all the buildings. It takes time and skill to scientifically trace the actual seismic incident apart from all its aftershocks back to its original place of origin.

I had left an earthquake's worth of damage in my wake … but it didn't just happen. And to be quite honest, this part of my story is still very hard to tell, but I know it is important that I tell it. This is my BDD.

I was born in 1964, the youngest of two sons of my biological dad. He and my mom divorced when I was very young, and unfortunately, my dad and I didn't spend very much time together when I was a boy. It was more of a visitation-and-child-support situation. At times when I was still pretty young, even when he would come to visit, I was so used to being with my mom that I didn't want to spend time with him.

But as I grew older, my older brother and I developed a stronger relationship with him through visitation and telephone calls. I found myself really missing him, especially when I started playing baseball. I always wished he would be able to come to one of my games, but it never happened.

Even so, he never stopped taking us to his house for visitation. We fished and camped together, something I really enjoyed. He also introduced me to my other family on his side, whom I fell in love with. I have vivid memories of moments at the end of our visitation on Sunday nights, wishing we could stay with him longer because we loved camping and fishing but also because of what was waiting for us back in our home. Dad often asked us if we were okay with the new stepdad situation—we always just said "yes" out of fear for what our stepdad might do to us if we said no but also out of fear of what Dad might do if he found out the truth. We didn't want our dad to get into trouble by taking matters into his own hands, especially against a police officer.

For these reasons, we kept quiet about our nightmare,

You see, my mom remarried when I was about six years old. The man who became my stepdad was a captain in the local police department. After we moved in with him, I would have given anything to stay with my real dad, mainly to escape the monster that my mom had married. From the time they said, "I do," he began viciously beating my mom and some of us kids. Of course, since he was a policeman—and a high-ranking one at that—my mother believed the lie that no one who would believe her if she reported him. She may have been right.

So, for about seven years, we just lived in hell.

My stepdad was an alcoholic, and he was most violent when he was drunk. He had two sons from a previous marriage, one of whom he rarely touched, mainly because he was old enough to fight back. That son eventually went into the Navy, but my other brothers and I weren't so lucky.

When he wasn't drunk, our stepdad was like a drill sergeant, so we had to learn to try to say the right thing at the right time. For the most part, we didn't speak unless we were spoken to. If he directly asked you a question and you gave him the right answer, he was your best friend. But if you gave an answer he didn't like, he'd knock you across the room. I think he really believed these were the best ways to raise boys up into manhood, but all he was doing was making sure that when the boyhood pain reached full maturity, there would be a hellish amount of it just looking for an outlet.

My stepbrother who was closest to me in age was less than a year older—and he got the worst of it. I think this was because he was overweight, so my stepdad constantly ridiculed and abused him for being lazy. Sometimes he would be getting beaten so badly that I would throw myself into the beating as well, just to give my brother some relief.

After they were married, my stepdad and my mom had another son, my younger half-brother. My stepdad never beat him that I was aware of. He was the kind of alcoholic who would beat you and then come back apologizing for it three hours later. That would last for maybe three or four days, or maybe even a week, before he would come back and do it again. He had a sense of remorse, which must have meant that he knew what he was doing was very wrong. But he would tell us not to tell anyone outside our house, especially since he was always promising that it would never happen again.

When I was very little, I learned where every hiding place in the house was so that when I heard him coming, I could try to escape his wrath. The best place to hide was in these little hidden compartments under our steps. As far as I remember, he never found me there.

My mom worked an afternoon shift at her job. I have a distinctive childhood memory about a certain day when my stepdad was home. I remember running out to Mom's car in tears, begging her to take me with her to work. I promised I would just sit in the car and be quiet—"just please don't leave me at home with him." I can't imagine how hard that was for her, but she had to leave me behind. When I turned back around toward the house, he was standing in the door, waiting to beat me for my cowardly outburst.

Once when he was giving me a talk about the dangers of drinking and driving, he tossed a few pictures from a police file on the table in front of me. They were photos of a couple of bodies that had been decapitated in a car accident. "So this is what happens when you drink and drive," he said. I never drank and drove my entire life. Those pictures are still so vivid in my head.

My poor mother got it worse than the rest of us. My stepdad would get off work and head to the bar until about two or three in the morning. From my room, I could hear what happened next. He would stumble into the house completely drunk. My mom would have the door locked, knowing what was coming. After a lot of yelling, he'd finally kick the door in and the sounds that came next still haunt me to this day. It sounded like yelps from a scared, injured little puppy.

And there was *nothing* I could do about it.

WHEN THE POWERLESS SEEK POWER

I want to be very clear here. I am not blaming my stepdad or saying the abuse I experienced from him either caused or justified my evil actions some years later. I was not the only one who was abused in my home, but I was the only one who loaded up a rifle and opened fire into a hallway full of students.

I am the only one responsible for the thing that only I did—and I have spent a lifetime feeling the weight of my actions. My regret is still heavy, even though my redemption has been so liberating.

But since this is my story—and since I am writing this in the hopes that it will help others to either share their story in a healthy way or be more mindful of what's happening in the lives of people around them—I just can't see a justifiable way to leave out the fact that I was abused so severely and for so long.

I am new to sharing this part, but it must be shared … lives may be hanging in the balance.

The abuse conditioned my mind to stay in a broken place all the time. I was very angry, and yet I was helpless to do anything. This made me feel even more weak and insecure, which only made me angrier. It was not just a vicious cycle in the metaphorical sense; I was literally caught in a cycle of viciousness with no way out.

That is, until I thought of one.

As I said before, "Doomsday" was not the first time I had contemplated or even attempted suicide. As a kid, killing myself eventually became the only tangible way I could imagine that would not only get me out of the hell I was living in but would also seemingly restore to me a sense of power and control. I had a say over nothing in my life, but taking my own life would let my stepdad forever know that I was brave and powerful—and in a way that he could never hurt me again. No one knew that inside of me, a battle was raging between living in a world of dysfunction and not living in this world at all. In my desperation, it felt like I could only have one or the other.

When I was twelve years old, I began flirting with death. I hadn't necessarily decided to actually follow through with it, but I went through the motions of hanging myself. I found a rope, put it up over the branch of tree, tied it around my neck, and stood up on a chair. I danced around a bit and rocked the chair, just feeling the exhilaration of life so close to death. I even went as far as writing a mock suicide note—acting out every part of the experience except the actual hanging. I just wanted to feel anything but victimized and out of control, even if only for a moment.

What felt like death had taunted me every day, so I began taunting it back.

Of course, no one knew what I was doing, and it had to stay that way or I would be beaten even worse. As soon as I had gotten the experience out of my system for the moment, I felt overwhelmed by the fear that someone would find the note, so I ran as fast as I could to tear it up so no one would ever find out how I was truly feeling or what I was truly doing. I just kept burying the pain deeper and deeper, not realizing it was actually growing a large root system within me ... and that someday, it would break through the surface in a terrifying way.

Relief That Doesn't Relieve

It wasn't an easy decision, but my mom finally divorced my stepdad when I was about fourteen. I know it might be easy for you to think ill of her because she let us stay in that situation for so long, but the truth is, my mom is my hero. She was just as terrified and trapped as the rest of us. She was just trying to hold us all together—and though I know she carries her own degree of guilt, despite me telling her that it is not necessary, the truth is she did her very best in an impossible situation.

After the divorce, she became a different person—the person she was never allowed to be in her abusive marriage. Her faith took a central role in her healing and in the details of her life. In fact, it was faith that helped her finally leave my stepdad. She had an aunt who was almost 100 years old who finally asked her, "How much longer are you going to take this abuse? Why are you going to let Satan have another moment of your joy?"

These loving, honest words caused something within my mom to come to life. She suddenly saw that the faith of her parents and family was still there, beckoning her to return to a place of safety and belonging. Since my stepdad was the captain of the precinct, he made pretty good money, and my mom had grown accustomed to the security she felt in the lifestyle they were living. Big house. Success. Notoriety. But she was suddenly able to see the complete madness of it all. She could no longer tolerate the life of an abused trophy wife— he had done too much damage, and she had finally had enough.

She never remarried. Her focus fully shifted to her faith and to the ominous task of taking care of her children. She worked three jobs and eventually started her own real estate company. She leaned back into her faith as the source of her ongoing healing. She wanted us to do the same, but I wanted nothing to do with what she was saying. In fact, at times it felt like she was trying to shove her religion down my throat. I just rolled my eyes because if there was a God who would let all this happen to us, I wanted no part of Him.

I was not one of those people who cried out to God for help … I hated Him and everything He loved, including myself.

Mom started going to a church just down the road from us pastored by a guy named John Bonds—the same pastor who came to visit me in the detention center after my arrest. No doubt he remembered the situation our family had been through years before. Mom made us go to a Sunday School class taught by a guy named Paul. He would take us kids to McDonald's every Sunday, which was very cool. In fact, I actually started enjoying church for a time simply because it also meant I got to go to McDonald's. It was also one of the few moments in life that I got to live in a world outside my family drama.

Mom wanted me to be saved so badly. She wanted to make up for lost time—to see all us kids healed from the past. She even tried to have me baptized, but I was in full, hardcore rebellion at that point. She did it all in love and gentleness, but I was just too angry to give in. She even sent us away to Christian weekend events, hoping that something would get through to us. At the time, nothing felt like it was reaching me at all.

I didn't like the person I was becoming, but I felt powerless to stop it. Once again, I was powerless. Such a great deal of damage had already been done inside me that I was caught in an inescapable pattern of anger, self-loathing, and destructive behaviors.

About a year after the divorce, when I was fifteen, I decided to play with the idea of killing myself again, but I took it a little further this time. While working a job at a local restaurant, I drank some of the bleach used to clean the floors. No one knew I did it. Obviously, it wasn't enough to kill me, but it did make me very, very sick. I recovered in secret and let no one else know just how much I was flirting with the idea of death.

I was so angry. What should have been "normal" moments of teenage adventure and angst would instead mushroom into something much larger and more dangerous … like "mushroom cloud" levels. One of those factors was a girlfriend. Early news reports of the school incident exaggerated the role this relationship played in the event. I did not go shoot up the school because a girl broke my heart. Not in the least. Now you can see that this rage and desire for destruction had been building in me for over a decade of my childhood.

I began a relationship with a girl while I was in high school that eventually became physical. As a young man who had been physically abused for so long, I think the sexual contact with someone who seemingly cared for me probably brought up quite a few feelings that I didn't exactly know how to handle. I had been robbed of so much, but I had her, and no matter how bad life might have been, at least we were together.

Until we weren't.

As often happens in high school relationships, one day she said she didn't want to see me anymore. I imagine she had really solid reasons for breaking it off that I just couldn't see at the time. I wanted to know if it was another guy, becoming insanely jealous and demonstrating that in my young adulthood, I was no longer a powerless victim who couldn't take action when he was hurt.

I became enraged, chased down two guys who I thought might be involved in her reasoning for breaking up with me, and beat them up. At that point, I went from being the one who was bullied to the one doing the bullying. Soon after, I chased another guy down a back road at 120 miles an hour at about 1 a.m. He finally pulled into the mall parking lot and I got out of my car and literally put my fist through his driver's side window. I dragged him out and beat him up as well.

I was done being passive. I was done losing things that were important to me. Obviously, after my girlfriend found out what I had done to those other guys, we were completely done with no hope of reconciliation. All of this happened about a year and a half before "Doomsday." The seeds of pain and abuse within me had finally broken through the surface—and I was making horrible choices out of the fruits of that tree.

By the time I walked into the school with a rifle, I was already dead. I felt like a little dog that had been beaten over and over again with the intent of making him into a mean dog. You beat him long enough—push him far enough—and you can never turn him back. Somewhere in his inner constitution, he'll always be a killer. At that point in my journey, I wasn't just in the pattern of *doing* something bad. In my heart of hearts, I was *becoming* something bad.

However, my desire to inflict pain was still mostly confined to hurting myself, which brings us to the pivotal question of why I did what I did at a school. Why hurt others instead of just hurting myself? Again, my original plan was not to hurt anyone but myself. Even those many months before when I attacked those other guys out of teenage jealousy and insecurity, there was never a desire within me to inflict mass destruction on people.

But the night before the school incident, the voices in my head connected some sinister dots, revealing an evil picture in my mind of what could be. It had never occurred to me before, but I can see now that I was a prime candidate for such a nefarious thought to take root and grow quickly.

If I'm being honest with myself, finding the peace—or more accurately, a resolution of the pain that was torturing me—was tied to retribution for the wrongs that had been done to me. My abuser was an authority figure in every sense of the word. He was my stepdad. He was a policeman. He was the captain of the precinct. According to all that seems right in this world, he should have been our protector, not our abuser. That little six-year-old who thought he was gaining a new family should have been able to feel completely safe in this man's home.

It was the most severe kind of breach. It unhinged something within me, disconnecting me from the innocence that every child should possess, along with the cluelessness that he or she possesses it in the first place. It should just *be*. Not only *was* something terribly wrong, but I also *knew* that something was terribly wrong—and both of these realities wounded me deeply. Sure, there is no such thing as normal, but there absolutely is such a thing as healthy. My childhood was neither normal nor healthy—and I felt like a fish out of water. I didn't know how to breathe.

It was not just that my stepdad had merely broken some rules of society. Kids don't really *see* the rules of safety and security through these kinds of lenses. Instead, they *feel* these boundaries very deeply, especially when they are crossed. Though I couldn't process it or express it in these kinds of words at the time, it was as if he broke the very laws of the universe, or at least of *my* universe.

This gross abuse of authority by someone who should have embodied its best parts left me with a sense that a great wrong needed to be atoned for. For the longest time, the best way

I could think of demanding this payment was with my own life. Such a drastic move would leave no doubt, especially considering the note I would leave that would expose my stepdad's cowardly actions. But the voices convinced me that I could right an even bigger wrong—the universal wrong.

I could leave a note the whole world would have to read.

If I were to act like a monster, then the world would finally know what my own monster had done to me. I know that it is a twisted line of reasoning, but I *was* twisted. If you don't value life for yourself, how in the world can you value the life of another person? My own lack of self-worth completely overshadowed the value of the lives of all the innocent people I would threaten.

All I could feel was a big, tragic story that could only be resolved with a big, tragic ending. By carrying out such an outlandish and devastating display of violence, I would destroy my stepdad and his power over me. I would finally show him what he had done by what I would do to them— and somehow, their blood would be on *his* hands as much as mine because he would know he was responsible for making me into this monster. But he wouldn't be the only one who would know—I would finally show them all exactly what a monster he was.

They would see his monster in me.

There is an old Martina McBride song called "Independence Day" about a battered woman who finally has enough and sets fire to her home, killing her abusive husband. I've always resonated with that song and video—I think that was where I was, even though I no longer lived with my stepdad and even though the actions I took wouldn't have exacted revenge against him directly.

I was ready to burn the world down.

Exposing the Shadows

When I finally stood before the judge, my attorney brought the details of my childhood to light. By that point, my stepdad had moved on to another job in another city. Again, you have to remember the times we were living in. There had certainly been school shootings, but most of them were personal acts of rage against specific people for specific reasons. A jealous ex-boyfriend taking revenge on the new beau. A troubled student attacking the teacher who gave him a bad grade. A bullied kid finally pushed too far who tracked down his bully to settle the score.

But for the most part, it was uncommon for someone to open fire on *everyone* in a school. This meant that the collective attitude, at least in my opinion, was different toward people like me. Don't get me wrong: people thought I was a maniac who should be locked away for life—and I agreed with them. But there was also a sense of curiosity about what had happened to me that might have caused me to do something so incredibly reckless.

I'm not saying that everyone had empathy for me; I'm only saying that because what I did was relatively unheard of, there seemed to be a greater desire to find out if there were reasons why I had come to this point. To that end, various people actually stood up in the court to speak on my behalf, and they weren't confined to family members. I remember one policeman in particular, a member of the bomb squad, who promised the judge, "You will never have to experience Mr. Stevens in your courtroom ever again." This man had known about the abuse his boss had been inflicting upon our family all those years.

The fact that people knew and didn't step up to intervene was definitely wrong—there is no excuse for it. However, you do have to understand it was also a different time. This is not a dismissal; rather, it's a contextual reality. In fact, even after the abuse was exposed to the judge, there was no punishment for my stepdad. The papers didn't report on it, though I'm not sure they really knew the whole story.

Even now, I struggle to reveal all of this because, believe it or not, I do not want to soil my stepdad's reputation. He is still alive and asked me to forgive him some time ago, which I did. I have been forgiven for too much to withhold forgiveness from him or anyone else. That's just not the guy I am anymore.

Regardless, I simply cannot find a way to tell this story without including this painful part, which includes him. I think this part matters. Even so, I haven't included my stepdad's name on purpose. I'm not trying to punish him, not in the least. I'm trying to help some kid or family out there who is facing a similar situation. This is just my story, not an exposé.

I did a horrible thing. It was my decision. I am responsible for it. Were there things that contributed to it? Yes. Do they excuse what I did? No. But should they be a part of the story? Probably.

You see, the same is true of my stepdad. He did a horrible thing, but nothing ever comes out of nowhere. He has a story, too, and I really don't know what hell he went through to become an abusive alcoholic. This doesn't excuse his actions, but it should keep us from not even trying to understand him. It is all too easy to vilify before we try to understand. Yes, there is no excuse for domestic abuse. None. But I only want you to understand the honest way I feel towards my abuser, as well as why I am including this part of the story now.

I think the truth is that no one sets out to become an alcoholic or someone who hurts other people. Growing up around the police force, I had a front-row seat for how stressful and mentally taxing the job really is. At times, it seemed like it was killing him. I'm not sure how or when he began turning to alcohol to cope, but the weight of his job was not light.

As I will discuss more, I sometimes speak to SWAT and police groups. What a difference forty years makes, right? I often address the stress they take home with them and how their reactions to it or their methods for coping with it can affect the little boys and girls in their homes. Alcohol. Drugs. Verbal abuse. You can usually hear a pin drop during this part of my talk because I think it really resonates with these men and women.

Just to leave no doubt, I think our law enforcement officers are nothing less than heroes. I know this is a huge topic of discussion today, especially with too many isolated incidents of police officers abusing their power in the name of corruption, racism, or bias. The misguided individuals who make these tragic choices should have to answer for them, just as I had to answer for mine.

But I don't think the actions of these individuals—which again, have been *way* too many (one is too many)—represent the entire law enforcement community. The tragic events of 9-11 revealed the more accurate assessment of law enforcement as a whole: they are heroes who are willing to risk their lives at a moment's notice to preserve, protect, and defend the lives of Americans ... *all* Americans. It should be okay to hold bad apples accountable for their rogue decisions, even if this leads to more widespread changes in policies and procedures to help deter and hopefully eliminate corruption and abuse of police power. But we should be able to do so without implying or outright saying that the entire bunch of apples is completely bad.

Police officers are just people too, even though they have taken an oath to put their own lives on the line for others. In my stepdad's case, he crossed a line that he should never have crossed, regardless of his level of stress. This difficult truth about my upbringing seemed to affect the judge at my trial. There was also no excusing what I had done, but he seemed to think that my actions didn't necessarily occur "out of nowhere."

After having entered the detention center facing up to 144 years in prison, I was found guilty and sentenced to four and a half years. The fact that I had not actually hurt anyone made a big difference. There were plenty of people in town who were outraged that I was not dealt with more harshly—and I understood their frustration. The whole thing was just as much of a surprise to me as to anyone else.

The other factor that was seemingly obvious to everyone present, even if they didn't quite understand how or why, was that by the time I stood before that judge, I was not the same young man who had been wrestling with demons in the darkness of a troubled mind six months earlier. I did not tell the judge what really happened to me that day—that is, about the light from the cross and the hand. For that matter, I didn't tell my attorney or my family, either. In my mind, my life was still about to be over and I would never again see the light of day, so the last thing I needed in that moment was a story that might very well cause everyone to come the conclusion that my cornbread wasn't quite done, if you know what I mean. Like most defendants, I was heavily coached regarding what to say and not to say, so I just kept to myself as much as possible and said only what I was instructed to say.

In the end, I was shocked that the sentence was so short, though four years of one's life is certainly nothing to sneeze at. I felt relief, but again, it was not the kind that truly calmed the enormous storm of pain, anger, and self-hate within me. Good things were happening to me, but I still couldn't see just how much Someone was looking out for me at every turn. I just kept making the turns, oblivious to it all. I may have been in less trouble than I thought, but there was no doubt I was still very troubled. And quite honestly, I was terrified to go to prison for any amount of time.

I was not yet a man of faith, probably because I still was so far away from believing that real forgiveness and real grace could be for me. I was just too bad of a person, as everyone now knew. I was famous in my hometown for the worst of things. I was the monster that everyone feared and hated. How could someone like that ever really change his stripes?

If we go back to the story of the naked guy who lived out among the tombs, the next part is often left out—the pigs always seem to take the cake, so to speak. After Jesus rendered him clothed and in his right mind, the man asked permission to join Jesus and His disciples as they traveled from town to town. After all, there were thousands of people following Him most everywhere he went.

But Jesus told him "no," which really surprises me. I kind of always thought that Jesus welcomed, encouraged, and even commanded people to follow Him. Why would He not let the guy upon whom he had just performed quite possibly the most radical miracle in all of Scripture to become part of His traveling crew? Just think of all he could continue to learn from Him on their journey. It just doesn't make sense.

I'm no theologian, but I think it may have had something to do with the fact that the people from that town were afraid of Jesus, and quite frankly, angry at Him because He had let all those pigs die. There was a lot of money lost that day for the sake of a man no one really wanted to redeem, much less be around in the first place. Scripture says that the townspeople actually *asked* Jesus to leave. They not only wanted nothing to do with the man; they also wanted nothing to do with Jesus.

But Jesus wasn't done with them. He still valued each of them as much as the man he had just changed. So he turned to the man and said, "Return to your home, and declare how much God has done for you ..." (Luke 8:39 ESV) In other words, Jesus sent him where He Himself was not welcome to go.

I guarantee that considering all this guy had done to terrorize the people in that town, along with all the embarrassing things they knew about him (remember, he was the "naked guy"), going back home was probably the *last* thing he wanted to do. But this was Christ's plan for him, so he did it anyway.

I feel his pain. Coming clean—that is, walking back into the spotlight to tell my appalling yet redemptive story—is really the last thing I want to do either, but I know that God cares about the people in the little and big communities around this nation (like Columbine, Sandy Hook, Parkland, and many more) who feel terrorized by people like me.

But unlike the man from the tombs, when I was sentenced to prison, I still wasn't ready to talk about "how much God had done for me," mainly because I still didn't know who God really was.

But that was about to change.

CHAPTER 6

Life (Unexpected) behind Bars

After my conviction and sentencing, I was transferred to Mecklenburg Correctional Center, where I would begin to serve my prison sentence. Mecklenburg was a maximum-security facility that, at one time in its history, housed the male death row for the Commonwealth of Virginia. It was constructed with the intention of housing the "worst of the worst" in the Virginia Department of Corrections system.

It met and exceeded expectations.

Even though my sentence wasn't nearly as bad as it could have been, I was still considered one of the worst of the worst. In fact, because of the nature of my crimes, my time in Mecklenburg was mostly spent in solitary confinement—that is, I lived in a cell by myself.

To be quite honest, I think this isolation was a blessing in disguise. I saw some very bad things in prison. I saw men get raped. I also saw men get shanked to death with makeshift weapons. It was a terrifying place, so I was grateful to be left to myself in my own cell, even if it was because they thought I was unstable and dangerous. The shower was the place I feared the most, but because of my age and crime classification, I was ordered to shower alone with a standing guard. The terrible reputation that had been weighing me down with so much shame was also somehow creating for me a strange advantage in my new arrangements.

Even so, my fear of not seeing the light of day became somewhat of a reality, though not a permanent one. In my cell, there was no natural light except what crept in from a tiny slit in the ceiling. I spent most of my time each day in this cell, but for one hour, I was put into a pit with a cage on top. It was not plush, and it sounds like something out of a movie, but I was not being put into the "hole" because of bad behavior. My hour in the hole was my recess—and from the bottom of that pit, I could look up through the bars of the cage above me and see the full sky. Never underestimate the power of a glimpse of freedom to someone who feels they will never experience it again for themselves.

Life in prison was a different universe altogether. During the six months I spent at the detention facility, I had learned quite a bit about surviving. I knew you were either predator or you were prey, so even though I was so young, I was determined to look the part of someone no one wanted to mess with. This was a new environment, and I knew I had to make an impression early on, just as I had done back at the detention center.

Solitary confinement took care of a lot of it, but even so, one of the first things I did was shave off all my hair, just to toughen up my appearance as much as possible. The other thing I did was dedicate much of my time to working out. I had started lifting weights constantly in jail, where they were more available in general-population settings. Solitary confinement kept me from lifting weights at Mecklenburg, but I still constantly did any kind of workout I could fathom inside my cell—pushups, sit-ups, chin ups, and the like. You wouldn't be able to tell it today, but I became very buff during this time, all in the name of self-protection and reputation.

As I will unpack, I later was moved to a different prison and out of solitary. In general, my scare tactics seemed to be working because I avoided a lot of the horrible things I had seen happen to other people. Besides the guy threatening to kill me in the psych ward, miraculously no one else really tried to take me out, which was very rare in the prison culture. For the most part, I was left alone, even though so many horrible things were happening all around me.

I tried to give off the vibe that I was a force to be reckoned with. I was the quiet guy everyone knew had snapped before, which meant I could snap again at any moment. If there was a scuffle and I was near it, I tried to stay out of it, which meant not jumping in to help someone who is getting ganged up on. I'm not proud of this, but I was a nineteen-year-old just trying to survive. I learned to keep my mouth shut, stay to myself, and do my job, which meant doing what the guards wanted.

Staying out of trouble was really my only job—and my paycheck was surviving another day.

In retrospect, I know that God protected me in prison. It wasn't just a matter of my tough exterior and mysterious demeanor. I just tried to blend in and not draw attention to myself. Slowly, my good behavior earned me more and more tiny privileges with the guards. I also made some friendships here and there. While there were some truly evil people within those walls, there were also some truly innocent people within those walls.

Some inmates were willing to hurt or kill anyone around them because, after all, they were already lifers and had nothing to lose. But most of the guys in prison were just pawns in a larger game, moved and passed around the board so that someone else—a guard, another inmate, a gang leader, you name it—could get whatever they wanted. A lot of these pawns were good guys who had their minds focused on staying out of trouble, getting their lives turned around, and getting back to their families.

Speaking of chess, there were large cracks in the walls on the backside of my cell at Mecklenburg through which I would pass a paper chessboard back and forth to the guy in the cell next to mine. We would draw our next move on the chessboard, going back and forth to pass the time. It was a little piece of civility in a very uncivilized place.

The political and economic structures inside prison were realities I learned to use to my advantage. Fear and trust were the foundations for avoiding trouble and gaining influence. Cigarettes were currency.

We would buy and sell things with one cigarette, two cigarettes, a pack of cigarettes, or whatever the appropriate corresponding value might be. I actually had this wooden box that was all hollowed out inside. It contained secret pins that created hidden compartments within. Since you were only allowed to have a certain number of cigarettes before they were considered to be contraband, most inmates would find creative ways—like these boxes—to store up a little extra power and influence.

The guards would eventually discover whatever method you used, but it would usually take multiple searches, which meant you had kept currency for a lengthy amount of time. As they say, necessity is the mother of invention.

A Sliver of Light

The visitors who had come to see me fairly regularly in the detention center trailed off pretty quickly when I was sent to Mecklenburg. It probably had to do with the finality of the whole thing—the fact that I was finally convicted and sentenced. I was about to go away for a long time, and like it or not, everyone else's lives on the outside were still going to move forward without me. Time would not stand still, even if it was about to slow down significantly in my world.

But above all, I think the distance deterred a lot of regular visitors. Mecklenburg was almost four hours from home. There was a church service at the prison led by a chaplain. Even though I still didn't really feel that anything God-related could ever be related to me, I did attend. After all, I had little else to do to occupy my time.

The other key influences in my life, in more ways that I realized at the time, were the trustees. A trustee was an inmate who no longer had to experience prison in the same way as all the other inmates. Trustees assisted the chaplains in handing out Bibles, pamphlets, and other literature to the inmates through the openings of their cell doors. They were able to move about the prison freely because they had earned the right to do so through good behavior and above all else, never trying to escape when they had the chance to.

Of all the ministers who had come in and out of my life up to that point, the trustees impacted me the most. They were a part of the prison ministry and would talk to me through my cell door about the love of Christ. I didn't get it at first—I was still so steeped in self-loathing. But since we had nothing but time and since, as inmates themselves, they had at least a basic understanding of what it felt like to be me, I felt like I could trust the trustees.

I would sit on the floor of my cell and listen as they read Scripture to me. I would then read the Bibles and pamphlets they would bring, even though a lot of it seemed over my head at the time. It took about a year of conversations and searching—a year of sifting through the jagged, wrecked pieces of my own heart—before something within me began to shift. We often say that something within someone "breaks," but I was already so very broken.

As much as my body was changing through all the working out I was doing in my cell, my soul was changing too. The outside was beefing up so I could intimidate others and defend myself, but the inside was beginning to soften. I began to have hope that I wasn't alone in this young life I had ruined. I never told any of the prison ministry workers or trustees the real story of what had happened to me that day in the school. They never knew that they were watering something deep within me that had been planted in the most bizarre and undeniable of ways.

Less than two years before, I had wrestled with dark, satanic voices in my head that preyed upon my pain and weakness to exploit me for a terrible outcome. But now, I was wrestling in a different way. There were no voices in my *head*, but there was definitely a conversation going on in my *heart*. I didn't feel attacked, but I did feel that I was being pursued. Even my complete lack of self-worth didn't seem to deter whatever—or Whomever—this was who just wouldn't leave well enough alone and let me succumb to the fate I deserved.

I was beginning to believe it actually might be Jesus.

During my time in prison, I saw some of the "jailhouse religion" that people often talk about when they refer to faith behind bars. This entailed men who would do the pious dance of pretending to be changed by Christ so they could make a better showing at their next parole hearing. For me, I really wasn't mature enough to think that far down the road. I was just beginning to be shocked by the possibility that Jesus was real and that it was either His own hand or the hand of one of His angels that had literally kept me from dying.

One night, I decided I was done running from my Pursuer. After being shipped from jail to psych wards to a maximum-security prison, it was time to answer the invitation to begin being set free from all the things that were *really* keeping me imprisoned. At about 11:30 p.m., I got out of my bed and got down on my knees. I knew I could be reprimanded if the guards caught me out of my bed after lights out, but I just couldn't lie there anymore.

I had fought and hid and resisted for so long … I was ready to surrender.

I began begging God for forgiveness. My tough exterior melted, and I began weeping with full repentance, using the best words I could find to ask Christ to come into my life and do with me what only He knew was best. I thanked Him for physically saving my life at the school and for not giving up on me spiritually. I told him that I knew I deserved death but that I was ready to accept the fact that He had given me life.

Then my heart turned to the people I had hurt. This broke me in a way that felt strangely liberating. I began praying for the families of the students from Lake Braddock High School. I prayed for them over and over again. I prayed for hours, confessing every hurt, failure, and insecurity in my entire life.

I remember looking up through the cell bars that covered the small slit of a window at the top of my cell to see a full moon. There wasn't much room for light to get into that cell, but the moon was so bright that it seemed to illuminate everything. It was fitting that the light would finally find me and that it would only take the smallest of openings to change everything.

I continued to cry myself to sleep in my cell that night. They were not tears of sorrow, but rather tears of gratitude and a deep love for a Savior who would still love me even after

I had so greatly sinned against God, myself, and all the people I had hurt. Something was resonating within me that I'm not sure I had ever felt before, or at least for many, many years—certainly so long ago that I couldn't remember the feeling: hope.

It was a new hope—unfamiliar to my mind, but strangely familiar to my soul, as if this small feeling of something higher than the life I had always known was actually a sliver of what I was made for. It was as if I had found myself unexpectedly standing in the home in which I was born but had been ripped away from long before I could ever walk or talk. I had momentary flashbacks of hope—recognizable glimpses that weren't actual memories but impressions buried somewhere deep in my spirit by God.

People sometimes miss this very important part of what it means to truly experience new life in Christ. Religion can feel so distant and foreign to all the things we enjoy and hold so dear. A place you belong. A place where you are known. A place that is fun. Inviting. Relaxing. Exciting.

We just don't usually apply these sorts of descriptions to Heaven, much less to life in Christ here on this earth. I guess you could say that sometimes *the Good News* doesn't seem to us to necessarily be *the good life*. Even the thought of Heaven feels like some other planet with all the floating around on clouds and harp playing and thousand-year-long worship services. Heaven might as well sound like Mars to us, which is why even our children often talk about the fact that they really don't want to go Heaven that badly, or at least anytime soon. It just doesn't feel like home.

But what I felt for the first time that night and have continued to sense over the winding path I've walked ever since is that really knowing Jesus is the place where I feel, not like an alien or an outsider, but like I have finally joined the family I've always longed for ... the one that has been relentlessly searching for me all my life, even before I knew it.

This sense of belonging led me to be bold and pray some very specific things before I drifted off to sleep. "Father, I have shown You and the world what I am and what I have done with my life. The world wanted me dead, but I plead to You from this cell floor that what life I have left in prison, please take it all—all of it—and show the world what You can do with it. It is Yours. I lay it before Your feet. I love You, Lord."

Hope finally felt like home, at least for that night.

New Dreams and New Fears

They say that hope springs *eternal*, which was definitely true for me. But I also woke up the next morning to find that real hope also springs *in the here and now*. It is crazy to think that only a few months earlier, my sole, distant hope was that someday I might be freed from my prison cell ... and of course, it was not something I really believed was possible.

I knew that my sentence was only four and a half years long, but the regret of what I had done had set up in me like concrete—and it kind of felt like my feet had been hardened within it and I was destined to swim with the fishes. I was so young. So immature. So lacking in self-confidence and self-worth. It didn't matter what the judge had said; I thought I would never make it out of this hell alive.

But then, I came alive.

I didn't just hope for *my eternity* in Heaven someday; I began to hope for *my today*. It may sound elementary, but my greatest hope was that God might choose to use me in the prison ministry in some capacity—and my greatest desire was to become a trustee. They had made such an impression on me over the previous year leading up to that night in my cell that I suppose it made perfect sense for me to join them.

Of course, being a trustee had its advantages. Above all else, as the name implies, they had earned a certain degree of trust from the warden and guards. This meant they could move freely about the prison, something that at that point in my journey sounded like a distant dream. I knew it would take a miracle for this to ever happen because of the nature of my charges.

Even so, I had the audacity to dream now. Enough crazy things had happened to me that I figured I might as well keep an open mind. I continued reading the Bible and various devotions in my cell, talking with the trustees through my cell door and attending the chapel services each week.

Over time, things did change—just not as I expected. They reclassified my status because of good behavior, and I was transferred out of Mecklenburg to a minimum-security prison called Palatine. You would think I would have been grateful to have this change, but this new prison situation meant I would have to be a part of a general population of inmates. Though I was a believer, I still felt a lot of fear and insecurity, even as I continued to search for knowledge and wisdom as I tried to grow in Christ.

I suddenly felt like a lamb among wolves.

I was only there for a couple of months, so most of my memories of the place are really more like isolated impressions. Above all, especially compared to Mecklenburg, I remember the openness of it all. It was a "yard" type of prison environment, which meant that it had a large open area where the general population congregated for much of the day. This tended to help foster gang culture as the prevalent ethos because the openness allowed various rival gangs to more easily square off against each other. The mission was to see who could establish dominance, which was the foundation for gaining more resources within the prison, finding or offering protection from attacks, and generally perpetuating some semblance of a life—that is, of a *prison* life.

My heart was definitely changing, but my situation had just become much more dangerous. I still had no intent of joining a gang, mainly because I didn't want to be involved with the whole give and take of it all. I didn't want someone having control over me because it was the only way I could be protected. That was the arrangement most of the guys in Palatine had to come to with someone (or a group of someones) more powerful than themselves, just so they could have some sort of place where they fit into this mini-society.

I did not want to find my place among them. I wanted to remain a loner as much as possible, except for my continuing interaction with the prison ministry staff and trustees. My dream of becoming a trustee was growing with every passing day, but it still seemed to be a complete impossibility, especially since I was about start off my time in Palatine with what would be considered to be bad behavior.

Since this was a minimal-security prison, I obviously had a lot more time to access various "amenities" of the facility. The weights and equipment were located outside in the open yard, so I spent about six hours every day lifting and sculpting my body, trying to add as many physical deterrents as I could to any would-be assailants. It seemed to work for a few days, but it quickly became apparent that I was not going to be left alone—not without a fight, that is.

One of the most well-known inmates, who also happened to work out every day, began taking an interest in me. He started talking trash and generally posturing toward me in a threatening manner. If you're "well-known" in prison, it's usually not because you have excelled in watercolors or community service. He was a dangerous troublemaker, the kind of guy who would crush your skull with the weights while you were trying to lift them. As much as I had tried to lay low and blend in, I was obviously on his radar, which meant that it was only a matter of time before he was going to come after me in some way.

I never said anything back to him. I just played it cool until my moment presented itself. Then, much as I had done back at the detention center, I jumped him like a madman, making sure that as many people as possible saw me "snap." Since he was already well known as an instigator, he received stricter punishment from the guards—he spent a long time in the hole. But word traveled fast within those walls, and my little tirade seemed to do the trick. I gained credibility and the others mostly left me alone, mainly because they were wary about whether I might jump them next.Besides working out, I kept trying to learn and grow in my faith, just hoping to be a trustee someday. When you have nothing to do for years on end, yet you know you need to stay "healthy" and not just succumb to institutionalization, it's hard to know what to do every day. You know you need to be doing *something* just to stay active and out of trouble. Handing out Bibles and encouraging inmates with what little I knew about Jesus was the only thing I could think of, so I prayed that it might happen and worked toward that goal by trying to attend every Bible study I could, making myself as valuable as possible to the prison ministry leaders.

Even so, it really wasn't my faith that I was known for in prison. The facility had a lot of educational opportunities, vocational training programs, and other things to help prisoners find some sort of path to rehabilitation. It also had televisions in some of the common areas, just so they could keep some viewpoint of the outside world and hopefully want to do the work of returning to it someday as productive citizens.

Access to television may have been a good thing for some of the inmates, but it was bad for me because as much as I wanted to isolate myself from the general population, many of them had seen my name, my picture, and my story on the news. The whole event and my subsequent journey from arrest to trial to prison had made a huge media splash nationwide, but especially across the state of Virginia … and now it felt like I was drowning in the wake of what I had done. Even so, this probably is at least partly why I avoided a lot of the trouble that could have come my way: everyone knew that, at one point in time, I was a guy who had *seriously* lost it.

Because my story was all over the news, I was given the nickname "Hollywood." For a guy who was trying his darndest to separate himself from the crazy thing he had done—and the crazy person he felt he had been—the nickname and notoriety were uncomfortable and unwelcome. Yes, I was fine with a reputation that would protect me in prison, but this brought the tension of being known and completely identified by the act of evil that had put me there.

"Tension" is the right word for this journey of identity. Would I ever be known as anyone but a school shooter? I suppose this tension remains today, lest we forget the title of this book and the reason you are reading it. And I suppose much of the reason I am writing it is because I have come to find some peace in it—but thirty-five years ago, my "faith legs" were as shaky as a little fawn's, and I would remain pretty wobbly for years to come.

I was not necessarily wobbly about who God was and what He had done in my life, but I definitely was about my own identity and worth. I had been forgiven, but I had not yet been fully healed—and every time I heard someone call me "Hollywood," it just reminded me of the person I no longer wanted to be.

ANCIENT CELLMATES

Besides Saul, I have sometimes identified with another guy in the Bible named Joseph. His is a crazy story, but his sentiments toward his brothers at the latter part really stick out for me. "As for you, you meant evil against me, but God meant it for good, to bring it about that many people should be kept alive, as they are today" (Genesis 50:20 ESV). This is pretty much a snapshot of so much in my life, especially the part where someone did something horrible that was meant for evil.

In Joseph's case, his brothers were the perpetrators. Out of jealousy, they plotted murder against him—that is some serious sibling rivalry. To say that cooler heads prevailed would be a gross overstatement. Yes, one of the brothers did manage to talk the sibling mob out of actually murdering their little brother, but things still went pretty awry. They roughed him up, destroyed his favorite coat—which may not seem like a big deal, but it was a gift from their father and the most tangible thing Joseph had in life to remind him that he was loved and valued—and finally sold him to band of traveling slave traders who came their way by happenstance. To top it off, they covered up their whole conspiracy with a story about a wild animal obviously taking Joseph out, all to convince their aging father.

It was pretty messed up.

So thirty years later, when Joseph spoke such spiritually mature and inspirational words to them, it's easy to lose sight of all that had really transpired in the "real world." For Joseph, the near-murderous mistreatment from his own brothers was really just the beginning of his woes. As they watched him stumble off toward Egypt in chains, it was as if the whole matter was over for them. (Though the guilt of what they had done never left them, as we see by their fear of meeting him years later.)

But for Joseph, the story was far from "out of sight, out of mind."

His life went through a multi-decade sequence of bad to better to bad again to worse to just okay and finally, to unbelievable redemption. He became a slave to a high-ranking Egyptian official named Potiphar, rose through the ranks of the household servants to become the most trusted member of the staff, and after politely refusing his owner's wife's inappropriate sexual advances, was accused and convicted of sexual assault without even being given a trial.

Boom. Prison. And he had done nothing to deserve it.

For lack of a better term, Joseph showed himself so faithful in prison that he rose to the rank of Head Trustee. The jailer trusted him with everything but his freedom. And from his prison cell, he began to dream … I can relate to that. But his dreams were more than just hopes of a better future. His dreams were literal messages from God—vivid images and warnings about the future.

He also seemed to be able to know the meaning of the dreams people around him were having. Being the good friend that he was, he served two of his fellow inmates well by helping them understand the meaning of their dreams. He was spot-on in every detail; in one case in particular, his interpretation foretold not only a cellmate's freedom, but also his restoration to a position of prominence and influence in Pharaoh's court. (It didn't work out so well for the other guy.)

Joseph only asked for one thing from the friend who was leaving their shared hellhole for a bedroom in the palace: that he would remember his old buddy back in prison who had helped him and maybe mention him to someone in authority who could get his sentence either amended or dropped.

Adding insult to the long list of injuries in Joseph's life, his newly liberated friend completely forgot him, leaving him to continue to rot in prison while he himself experienced the opulence of life in the palace. Only years later, when Pharaoh himself had a dream that troubled him to the core—one none of his spiritual advisors or soothsayers could make heads or tails of—that the friend had an "aha" moment.

Hmm, why does this make me feel like I've forgotten something? Did I leave the stove on? Did I forget to check the oil in my camel? Hmm ... Oh crap! Joseph!

Pulled from the pits of prison, Joseph was cleaned up and presented to Pharaoh. After hearing his dream, God gave him the interpretation to a tee—and in one day, he was not only completely exonerated from all his bogus crimes, but also elevated to the highest political position in all of Egypt besides that of Pharaoh himself.

It is a literal "rags to riches" event ... a twenty-year, overnight success story.

If we rejoin the words Joseph spoke to his brothers from his throne in Egypt so many years later, perhaps we can begin to feel just a tiny bit of the miraculous transformation that has happened. How could a guy be so mistreated by the ones he should have been able to trust the most yet still have such a perspective, no matter how rich and powerful he had become?

I don't think it was the luxury of the palace or the respect of the people that changed Joseph's heart. His words reflected something much deeper, something only the intervention of a creative, supernatural Friend could explain. Joseph's words didn't demonstrate that he was without anger, bitterness, greed, or anything else of the sort. The whole story is really not about how good Joseph was, though his actions and attitudes can certainly inspire and steady us in hard times. The story is really about the way God allowed the evil done against Joseph not only to *not* detract from God's ultimate purposes in his life but to enhance them.

It's not that God sent the evil; it's that He wasn't deterred by it one bit. He took it and used it to add exclamation marks to the sentence He was already writing in His great book of history and eternity. It's just another incredible aspect of the mystery of God: He creates good from evil at a disproportionate level … the worse we try to make it, the better He can redeem it.

While I identify with Joseph's story because he was a jailbird like myself, I also struggle with it. You see, I am less like Joseph and more like the brothers who so viciously attacked him and sold him down the river (or desert, as it were). I'm not saying that Joseph didn't have any faults or didn't deserve anything bad ever happening in his life. He was human, therefore flawed. If nothing else, he certainly lacked wisdom and perhaps humility in his younger years when he had no qualms sharing his dreams (even though they ended up coming true) about his father, mother, and brothers all bowing down before him. That would make any older brother pretty upset, though obviously almost murdering him and then selling him into slavery was a pretty extreme reaction. Perhaps they just should have given him an epic wedgie and called it a day.

But stories like Joseph's, though they inspire us with faith, can also make us feel pretty distant from the hope of redemption that came into his life. After all, who among us feels as good and deserving as Joseph? Probably none of us ... and if we do, then we have other problems anyway. I have no doubt which characters look more like me.

The most revolutionary part of the whole story isn't what God did to redeem and bless Joseph; it is what God did to redeem and bless the brothers who had caused all the trouble in the first place. It is one thing to come to the rescue of someone who is wrongly attacked by a jealous family, falsely accused by authority figures, and wrongly imprisoned by foreign governments, but it is another thing altogether to come to the rescue of the jealous family, the authority figures, and the foreign government.

But this is exactly what God did in Joseph's story. The only reason his brothers ever found themselves in Joseph's presence was that they were in grave danger from a vast famine that threatened to wipe out their entire family. Joseph wasn't just a figurehead of authority; he was in charge of a multi-year, highly coordinated food conservation and storage project designed to basically feed the entire known world throughout the coming famine revealed in Pharaoh's dream.

When his brothers stood before him, it was to ask for his help, something they had not given him when he had begged for it years before. My bet is that Joseph's former master, Potiphar—along with the promiscuous wife who had tried to seduce Joseph years before—also ate from Joseph's feeding program. As did the slave traders who had bought him. As did the absent-minded friend from prison who forgot him.

My point is that God didn't just redeem the *good* guys of the story ... he redeemed everyone who was willing to receive His gift of food and provision. That was the part of God's story in my life that I just couldn't grasp at the time. I was certainly benefitting from His provision and rescue, but since I didn't think of myself as a Joseph, I just didn't put two and two together. I wanted to keep punishing myself for my great sins, even if only internally.

It would take years to figure out that this story wasn't solely about me, just as Joseph's story wasn't solely about him. This was about God's grand plan to offer redemption to everyone in the story, including heroes like Joseph.

And villains like me.

CHAPTER 7

Minimal Security

My time in minimal-security prison was full of ups and downs, but the best thing that ever happened to me within those walls was being informed that I was being transferred again. My prisoner status was again reclassified because of a combination of good behavior and various parole evaluations. None of these evaluations had led to my actual parole, but they did lead the authorities to downgrade the state's level of concern about the danger I posed to society. To them, it was becoming less and less likely that I would be another statistic in the staggering recidivism rates in this country.

This time, I was taken to State Prison Camp Number 26 near Haymarket, Virginia. I cannot begin to tell you what a transformative moment this was for me. It was still incarceration, but it was also a chance to be outside of prison walls every day. This situation did include hard labor, but it was a welcome change. I preferred to work out in the sun every day rather than sit in a cell or hang out in a prison yard waiting to be attacked.

We basically worked as road crews, much like in the old movie *Cool Hand Luke*. We would wake up early, eat a little chow, and then load up in the back of a big dump-type truck that had a special cab on the back made for prisoner transport. We would climb into the truck together with all of our chains and get locked down. We were literally a chain gang.

After a short or long ride, depending upon the day's work destination, we would unload and receive our orders for the day. Sometimes we would be tasked with clearing brush or overgrown weeds on the side of the road. We were given tools called weeders, which had long handles with horizontal blades at the end. You would swing that weeder until it was almost dark. It was hard work, but I much preferred it to anything else I had done in prison up to that point.

Another job was putting down and spreading gravel on various roads in rural Virginia. At first, our hands would get pretty blistered up—at least until the blisters turned to callouses from repeated use. As winter drew near, we were tasked with constructing long snow fences in Middleburg, Virginia, to help the snow pile up and stay off the main highways.

When the workday was over, it was back into the truck to head home to Camp 26. When we returned, it was chow, showers, and straight to bed—not that we had much energy to stay up anyway. We slept in a dorm. At first light, it was back up and at it all over again.

The nature of life in the camp was based upon a limited amount of trust; after all, you had to have advanced this far from previous stops to even qualify. For this reason, there were fewer dangerous shenanigans like attacks and gang activities. Doing such things would have earned any of us a one-way ticket back to a much less desirable prison experience.

One example of this opportunity to prove your trustworthiness was the procedure for going to the bathroom out on a job site. When you had to go, you would say to the guard, "Shake a bush?"

He would reply, "Shake a bush." Then he would escort you to the nearest area where there was a bush or tree. You would go behind the bush and for a moment, be out of his full sight. Thus "shake a bush" meant that it was your responsibility to keep shaking the branches while you went to assure him you were still back there. If the bush wasn't shaking, then the shotgun was suddenly something you had to be worried about. You haven't lived until you've had to do your business with someone holding a shotgun near you, waiting for you to finish.

On the work crew, we made ten cents an hour. I don't know how it works today, but back then, the state would charge $7 or $8 an hour for the services the inmates provided out on the work sites—which meant the state made about $7.90 an hour, and we would get about ten cents of it. Considering that I didn't deserve to see the light of day, I have always considered it to be an incredible opportunity.

This meant that, by the end of the week, you had usually earned about four or five dollars. We would take our earnings to the commissary to purchase essentials for the coming week—things like toothpaste or deodorant. Family members were also allowed to put money in our commissary accounts, which is generally how inmates could afford to buy cigarettes.

For me, life in Camp 26 was like a daily gift of freedom. Just walking out on the side of the road afforded me the chance to smell the open air and take in the bigness of life on the outside. Of course, roadside work had its downsides and dangers. Snakes were one hazard. If you came across a snake while cutting down the tall grass, which happened pretty frequently, you had to keep your cool and not run like any other "normal" human would. Out there, running meant you were escaping. So instead of running, you had to kill the snake with your rake or weeder, which meant you became pretty adept at knowing how to position yourself as you began cutting into a section of tall, overgrown vegetation.

But if you were smart, not running was just another part of the grander exit strategy to get out of prison altogether. Again, if you had made it this far, you were closer to parole than ever before. You had to discipline yourself not to abuse the small freedoms afforded you in an effort to force the ultimate freedom you wanted. It was like a piece of steak dangling before you that you knew you couldn't eat … unless you never wanted steak ever again for the rest of your life.

The guards would talk about having "rabbit in your blood." If you were skittish and tempted to run like a rabbit when you had the ability to do so, they would talk about the fact that you would have five more years added to your sentence each time you tried. If you had proven your trust up to that point, they would lengthen the leash, so to speak. Occasionally, I would find myself a tenth of a mile down the street with no gun trained on me.

Freedom seemed so close. I was tempted to take it, but it was only a test.

Trust and Freedom

I suppose I passed the test because at Camp 26, something happened I had only considered possible in my dreams: I became a trustee. Ever since Mecklenburg, this had been my highest aspiration, and now it had come to pass.

This meant I no longer loaded up with the others to work on the roads. There was a little office the size of a small hut that contained the chaplain's supplies. I would stay there, helping to prepare everything necessary for church services but also getting materials together so we could offer Bibles, pamphlets, and other handouts to the prisoners when they returned from work.

That little hut became a sanctuary to me.

I grew so much spiritually during my time as a trustee, mainly because I was able to serve others, but also because there was a radio in my little hut. I don't remember what radio station it was tuned to, but I do remember listening to J. Vernon McGee's program every day. He would break down the context, meaning, and application of Scripture in a way I had never encountered. I just soaked it up like a sponge.

As I have said before, very few things come out of nowhere—they come from somewhere within us, even if it's a place we don't know exists. This was a time in my life when an incredible amount of good things were planted within me, even though much of what would poke through the soil wouldn't do so for years to come. But you should never underestimate the power of a seed—the power of words of love, encouragement, and instruction spoken to those whom most have written off.

In that little hut, God's words spoken to me over the radio waves felt like they were revolutionizing my life.

Meanwhile, other unseen things related to my case were happening. Throughout my incarceration, my mother had always been supportive, as had other members of my family. Once I was in the camp, which was nearer to my grandparents, my grandfather came to visit me every Sunday. He would always bring me a little shoebox that my grandmother had prepared, filled with simple trinkets, cookies, candy bars, homemade sandwiches, and things like that. It would have to go through security, just to ensure that my kind old grandfather wasn't slipping me any files or pipe bombs. I always looked forward to that little box so very much—it was just a small piece of the outside world.

But just as this box brought me surprises each week, there were other surprises brewing in the Commonwealth of Virginia and its evolving policy toward younger felony offenders. The state judiciary authorities were launching a new alternative sentencing program for certain, very specific cases.

I was about to witness another actual miracle. I don't know why, but the Chairperson of the Board of Supervisors for Fairfax County had taken a special interest in my case. Working with my mother on the whole process, the chairperson wanted to pursue the possibility of letting me have a second chance at proving myself ... a second chance *outside* of prison altogether.

This process aligned with the fact that I was up for parole for a third time. The chairperson convinced the circuit court judge to take another look at my case—the same judge who had heard it the first time. With the new program as the backdrop, the judge allowed his recommendation to be a part of the presentation to the parole board. The request was that I would be sentenced to forty hours of community service under high supervision for five years. Of course, I would also be required to visit with a parole officer several times a week.

The county's reasoning was multifaceted. First of all, there were the many puzzle pieces related to my abuse by an authority figure and alcoholic. Second, no one had been physically hurt in my crimes. Plus, I was only eighteen years old when the incident occurred. Finally, I had been in prison for a while and had earned my way to trustee status. The authorities felt I could be a good test case for this brand-new program. I still had a lot to prove, but they thought I might do a better job of rehabilitating outside of prison.

Even though this was all completely legal, they still tried to keep the media from reporting on it. My story had been such a media firestorm that it could cause a public backlash that would harm the program moving forward.

If one of today's school shooters were to get this kind of treatment, my guess is there would be a public outcry. Though the state authorities were worried about that in my case, I don't think we're comparing apples to apples. The alternative release program was one of the state's ongoing efforts to better understand the actual causes, not just the symptoms, of why someone like me would do what I did at such a young age. Fast forward thirty-plus years through numerous horrors like Columbine, Sandy Hook, and Parkland, and the modern culture is much more dialed in on this issue … and rightly so.

I didn't deserve it, but I was very grateful for the possibility of living life out of prison.

So much had happened since the night I surrendered my life to Christ on the cold floor of that prison cell. I had originally believed I would probably never make it out alive. Yet God had a plan beyond what I could have ever dreamed— and obviously beyond what I could ever deserve. I left Camp 26 about six months after the night I accepted Christ's invitation. All told, I had been in prison a little over two years instead of the lifetime I originally feared. When you're young, years feel like decades, but now that I'm fifty-five, I can clearly see that I probably should've been sentenced to forty years, not four and a half years. I am so grateful for a second chance at life beyond bars with a new peace I never knew BDD.

I was leaving prison, never to return. At the time, I wasn't exactly a free man in every sense of the word, but I was most definitely free.

The New Sounds of a New Life

The program I was being paroled under required me to work under constant supervision for forty hours every week. After working this many hours and more in Camp 26, I was more than happy to do so with no one holding a shotgun near me. I would no longer have to "shake a bush" when I wanted to go to the restroom. I also wouldn't have to target the biggest guy in the room to make a statement to the others about my willingness and ability to fight.

I moved back in with my mother. It was surreal to have a normal bed again. To have normal conversations again. To walk outside whenever I wanted. Order a hamburger whenever I wanted. Drive whenever I wanted. For the most part, I could go anywhere I wanted, as long as I showed up on time for work, showed up for every meeting with my parole officer, and didn't leave the state without permission.

Mom and I began catching up on lost time. She was thrilled to learn that her prayers for me to come to faith had been answered, though I still didn't tell her about the hand experience at the school that day. It still just seemed all too much for people to believe, and I still didn't want to be branded a lunatic, especially now that I had a newfound chance at freedom. All she really knew was that I was a believer.

I also reconnected with other family members here and there, though I certainly felt that some of them treated me a little differently than before. I suppose there was no way that wouldn't happen. If I was in their shoes and a school shooter were to suddenly sit down across the table for a random family Sunday afternoon dinner, the conversation would be a little awkward at best.

I was out, and I was changed, but the whole thing still haunted me on an identity level. I felt an *inner transformation*, but I still couldn't escape the *outer existence*. To use biblical terms, there was new wine within me, but I still felt like I was an old wineskin. I felt that if I were to talk too much or too freely about what God had been miraculously doing in my life, people would chalk it up to jailhouse religion nonsense—or worse, they would think I was undergoing another break from reality, even if this departure didn't lead to such violent ends.

Then there was the guilt I felt for not fully paying the price my crimes demanded. It sounds counterintuitive to feel great gratitude and great guilt at the same time, but that was my reality. I was a changed man, but I was also a man still in the daily process of being changed, and sometimes the process of discovery and maturation can have its awkward stages. Just ask any teenager.

Most of us are familiar with the concept of survivor's guilt—that is, one person surviving a horrible experience or diagnosis while others who seemingly didn't deserve it suffered or died—but I was experiencing something else. It was more like perpetrator's guilt. Grace was so real and radical that I still had a long way to go in learning to receive it, much less express what it had done in my life. The layers of what was happening to me were many and complex.

The good news was that, while I wrestled with these existential questions of guilt, justice, identity, and grace, there was an external plan in place. I didn't have to sit around and ponder the depths of the universe, which would have no doubt sent me spiraling into a dark hole, perhaps even one of the dark holes I had visited before. God was gracious enough not only to set me free from prison but also to give me something to do that would occupy my time and my hands while I kept working through what everything in this new life really meant.

The job assigned to me was not just at a task; it became another life-changing part of my journey.

I had started playing guitar when I was about nine years old. I could escape into that for hours on end, so I had actually become pretty good for my age. The leaders from the alternative sentence program, who also considered input from my mother, took into account the fact that I possessed this skill when they began deliberating the next steps for my rehabilitation. Since I was one of the first people to be paroled under this new program, there were a lot of unique factors at play.

My assignment was to spend forty hours each week teaching guitar to children and youth at a special needs daycare-like facility in Fairfax County. It seemed to be an area where a young person like me, who still had some hope for a future outside of incarceration, could really find new and inspiring perspective by helping such an underserved population. The job had its own set of unique challenges, but I would find it to be incredibly inspirational and life-giving.

Sitting with a child who had trouble even saying his own name or feeding himself had a way of really putting my problems into perspective. I was sometimes unable to value myself because of the choices I had made, which sometimes led me to moments of self-pity and narcissism. Sitting with these precious kids had a way of snapping me out of that mindset pretty quickly. The openness of their hearts and the authenticity of their pure, unbridled joy over the process was like a breath of fresh air—one I didn't really know I needed but which always affected me after I breathed it in.

Even though the process was fulfilling, it was not an easy job. Not in the least. After all, it could never really be completed—my students were unlikely to go on to greatness in the music industry or even find a way to make a living at music at all (something I would discover later is almost impossible regardless of who you are). But teaching my kids to play guitar had a way of centering me in the present, focusing my mind and energies upon that particular lesson at that particular moment.

It helped make *now* seem just as important as *then*.

While there are masters who play lead guitar licks at a level beyond most normal musicians, there are basic guitar chords and bass notes that almost anyone can learn. There is an old story about a kid who asked his mom for bass lessons. After the first one, his mom asked, "What did you learn today?"

"I learned to play a G," he said.

The next week, she asked again and he responded with, "I learned a C." The third week, he said that he learned how to play a D.

The fourth week rolled around and his mother asked, "So what did you learn at practice this week?"

The boy shrugged and said, "Eh, I blew it off … I had a gig."

The point is that there are things that can be taught pretty simply and quickly to most people who want to play guitar. However, for my students, these rules didn't apply. It was slow going, which was to be expected, but was still somehow surprising when you had to endure it. Just because you know something to be true doesn't mean it doesn't affect you when you actually have to do it.

What came pretty easily to me on the guitar was not at all easy for them. It might take four hours to teach one of the kids a simple G chord. "Okay, one finger on this fret, this finger on this fret, and this finger here." It was all too easy to become lazy and just say, "Okay, third fret, one finger on all these strings … that will basically make the same sound." But even though I could have taught them "cheat" chords, I was always reminded of the truth that it wasn't the chords I was really cheating; it was those precious kids. They deserved better.

I would be lying if I said this process didn't frustrate me to no end at times. But through it, I began to learn patience— and that patience is more likely to grow and flourish within you when it is directed toward an actual person for whom you care and have empathy.

We treat things like patience as if they are concepts we can just invoke at any moment by the sheer force of our will. If you have road rage, you can try to keep it at bay by just breathing more deeply and slowly counting to ten. This may help treat the symptom but not the cause of the impatience. If you really want to learn patience, pull up next to the poor little elderly woman you just berated with your horn for the last three miles in traffic. Look at her and try to imagine what she is going through. How she is feeling. What she is scared of. What diagnosis or fear or challenge she may be facing.

In other words, see *her* and not just yourself. When you can do that—that is, see her as an actual person and not just an obstacle between you and your destination—you probably won't need those deep breaths as much. You will naturally be feeling and showing patience.

The very thing you hoped to gain through *self-discipline* can sometimes better be found through *others-discipline*. Life not lived in isolation, but rather *toward* someone outside of yourself, is the proving ground for continued maturity. Contrary to popular belief, you can't just set up camp in a library, the woods, a cabin, or on a beach with a stack of books and find complete enlightenment or personal transformation. We are obsessed with self-help, and while it most definitely can be beneficial in better understanding the ways we are made and the reasons for our actions and reactions, this knowledge has its limits in terms of application.

When you actually have to exercise patience for another real person in a real situation, it becomes easy to see the limitations of head knowledge. It's like knowing that a huge ice cream sundae is bad for you, which is all well and good until one is placed on the table in front of you. In that moment, knowledge isn't the only thing at play.

All the knowledge in the world can't change a heart. The postmodern assumption that most of us don't realize we believe is this: if we try hard enough, we can *learn* our way out of the human condition. We wouldn't necessarily say that out loud, but we live as if we can raise ourselves from this fallen nature if we just study harder, discipline ourselves more, and maybe are nicer to people we randomly meet.

For the most part, we are moving so quickly around this belief that we barely notice it. Back to the ice cream sundae. If you ate one at every meal for years on end, which would be really bad for you, you would eventually become used to it and you wouldn't think of it as "bad." At some point, to you it would just be "food."

I didn't know how badly isolation was affecting me, so God had to push me out of my comfort zone and into contact with others … and they became the best kind of nutrition for the young faith within me. In fact, in every aspect of my story, what God was teaching me didn't come fully alive in me until I had to experience it with others. In my "bunker," the light reflecting from the lady's cross necklace affected me, but in an irritating way. But it wasn't until several of my hostages engaged me directly, begging me not to kill myself, that my Rescuer showed up. The same thing was true with the teacher who refused to leave me. It happened again with trustees who cared enough to talk to me about the love of Christ through my prison cell door. At every turn, knowledge or a new understanding of something profound was a seed that only grew when it was watered by interacting with someone else.

This was never truer than with my guitar students. None of them ever opened up a book and instructed me on the finer points of theology. None of them ever quoted long passages of Scripture or drew me a Venn diagram that perfectly expressed the mysteries of the balance between soul and spirit. Yet I learned more from them than from anyone else in my life up to that point.

God had placed a *new heart* within an *old me*. This is where the epicenter of the great tension within all of us is found. The *experiences* of this life with the *people* of this life are the pathways by which a newness of heart spreads outward to the rest of one's life, displacing more and more of the old with something new. Again, it doesn't happen in a theological lab or in an intellectual vacuum. It happens by learning to be loved by God, by loving God in return, and by serving others with same love that God continually shows to you.

We have a huge, gaping hole where this simple truth should be. People hurt us, and we have no problem blaming them for our pain. But we rarely realize that, as much as the *wrong kinds* of relationships and experiences lead to deep pain, God also uses the *right kinds* of relationships and experiences with His people to heal us. This is certainly true on a Christian community level, which is why the Apostle James reminds us, "Therefore, confess your sins to one another and pray for one another, that you may be healed" (James 5:16 ESV). The "one another" here is a key to the real, present, and continual healing that we often miss. Sometimes, we confess only to God, which is a good thing to do in seeking forgiveness. But God has given us the gift of one another—and the right kind of interaction between us—to ultimately add to forgiveness ongoing, true healing.

But this is not only true on a Christian community level; it is true on any level. Though I obviously never technically confessed any of my sins to those precious kids, my long-term engagement with them, which launched me into the act of serving someone other than myself, began to produce moments of healing in me that I never could have found on my own. I couldn't have just willed such moments through more private introspection or contemplation, though both of these are essential. They just aren't essentials unto themselves; they are supposed to lead you to action, and there are very few actions in this life that do not affect others.

I had already been forgiven, but I wasn't yet done healing (and I'm still not). My wounds were deep, and shame still wanted to dominate much of my perception of myself. But when I was teaching those kids guitar chords, learning patience through the difficult process, and realizing that they all had much more of an uphill climb in this life than I did, I temporarily stopped feeling only like a former shooter and began feeling like a person who could serve others. I guess you could say that during these moments with those special-needs kids, I experienced beautiful, momentary lapses in shame ... and any relief was a welcome relief. I experienced some of the freedom that is found in self-forgetfulness.[1]

I eventually organized a talent show so my students could showcase their hard work and accomplishments, and I knew it meant a lot to both the kids and their parents. Little did I know that I was being prepared for much more event organization in my distant future. Even so, that particular talent show remains one of the most important, impactful events I have ever been a part of.

CHAPTER 8

The Role of a Lifetime

The job I got working with the kids was not exactly meant to sustain me. It basically only paid enough for spending money. But I was able to get another job working nights at TGI Fridays as a side cook. I honestly don't remember if they really knew I was a felon when they hired me. My best recollection was that I probably did not put it down on my application. It was something I did many times afterwards on job applications: leave that part blank. You must remember that this was still long before the days of nearly instantaneous digital background checks.

I suppose this is when I really began hiding in plain sight. My shame found an unwelcome friend, another stubborn stowaway that stuck with me for years: fear. I had beefed up in prison, physically assaulted some huge guys to prove my toughness, and survived on a chain gang, but I was still so very afraid, mainly that the outside world would realize who I was and take matters into their own hands to protect themselves from me.

Fear is simply not logical. We think we know that, but it is very difficult to remember it when we are looking one of ours in the face. While logic can help someone begin to work through his or her fear, you can't just dissolve fear with a solid argument about why you shouldn't be afraid. It doesn't work that way, and when we act as if it does, we become insensitive at best and dismissive at worst.

For example, I don't have a problem taking long flights on airplanes. It just doesn't hit that part of my brain or emotions. The reality is, my body is flying at hundreds of miles per hour in a metal tube several miles above the surface of the earth, and if I weren't in this tube, I would be freezing to death while unable to breathe. And if this tube suddenly has a mechanical failure—as many others just like it have—the fact that I fastened my seatbelt really won't matter because there will be no survivors when we all plummet into the hard earth below at literal breakneck speed. For whatever reason, none of these "facts" upset my emotional equilibrium enough to make me truly afraid of flying (although you may be second guessing it after my description).

But to someone who has a fear of flying, these facts are all they can hear inside their heads. And no matter how *you* view it, you can't just tell them not to feel how they are feeling and to rely on logic. Sure, you can remind them that statistically, an almost non-existent percentage of planes crash around the world each year, making it one of the safest forms of transportation. You can even try to show them how illogical it really is that they are less afraid of riding in a car than flying on a plane since it is more than a hundred times more likely they will be injured or die in a car crash than a plane crash. But this accurate data alone won't truly relieve them of the anxiety and fear of flying.

That was me. I was terrified of living out in the open. Yes, I had been miraculously rescued from certain death, miraculously protected in prison, and then miraculously released far sooner than I ever could have dreamed, but none of these "facts" had yet relieved me of my fear, which, of course, was tethered to my shame.

"You're the One!"

I was about thirty days out of prison and working my job with the kids and at TGI Fridays when someone invited me to attend a Bible study with some other older teens and young adults at an apartment in Arlington, Virginia.

I sat there in that small apartment next to "real" people, and it was one of the most surreal experiences I had ever had up to that point. We engaged in a Bible study and then we just watched television together. I pretty much stayed to myself, watching and marveling at the fact that I was there at all. There was a lot of joking around and cutting up, just as you would expect at such a gathering.

Everyone could tell that I was timid, but no one knew why. For a moment, there was a hint of hope not just for a life outside of prison but also for a productive life with friends and a community. Perhaps even a little bit of normalcy.

Just then, out of nowhere, an older woman walked down the hallway of the apartment from one of the back rooms. She took one look at me, and her entire countenance radically changed. Her face reflected some mixture of excitement and disbelief while I could feel my face becoming redder. Perhaps I had started dreaming of a "normal" life too soon because it was obvious something was up with this lady … and her main focus was the kid in the room trying to disappear into the background.

She pointed a trembling finger at me and yelled, "You're the one!"

My face went from red to white as my heart sank within me. "Hollywood" couldn't hide out in a Bible study—someone had recognized me, and my warm welcome was about to go ice cold in a hurry.

"You are the one!" she yelled again. I just knew she was about to tell everyone there what I had done, and then who knew how they would respond? They would all stare. The girls would shift away from me in fear. The guys might try to push me around to protect the others. This was a disaster.

I hightailed it out of there like a man on fire. I mean, I literally ran from that apartment as fast as I could. Little did I know, the woman who had yelled at me did not want me to leave, so she and some of the other friends ran after me into the parking lot. After a lot or coaxing and reassurance, I found out that she wasn't pointing at me because she recognized me from the news or from my mug shot. She was pointing at me because she recognized me from somewhere much stranger: her dreams.

Her name was Rita Warren. At the time, I had no idea how much she would impact my life. She was truly a remarkable lady, albeit not necessarily the best at first-time introductions. She was a small Italian lady who worked as a Christian lobbyist in Washington, DC. Among other things, she was pursuing a crazy dream, one that had led her to minister to many power brokers in the Capitol, including multiple members of Congress.

Once I had calmed down enough to actually hear what she was saying, she told me that she had spent the past four years organizing and negotiating for the approval of a large-scale, live Passion play that would happen literally throughout the DC area, culminating on the steps of the US Capitol Building.

President Ronald Reagan was in office at the time, and Tip O'Neal was the Speaker of the House. Despite the fact that so many high-ranking officials were strong people of faith, it was still a huge deal to even consider a religious event such as this in middle of the nation's public square. In fact, it would be the first time in history that such an event would be allowed on United States government property. Rita had devoted much of her life over the past four years to meeting with officials, writing proposals, and working to gain the necessary permits and approvals.

So, what did all this have to do with me?

Rita was overwhelmed with emotion because she said that God had given her a vision in her dreams, specifically that a young man would come to her who would play the part of Jesus Christ in front of the entire world. God told her that she would know him when she saw him.

Apparently, she had just seen him … when she saw me! She said that I was the one God had promised in her dreams to play this part. Talk about someone who had gotten her lines crossed; this lady had gotten her lines tied up in knots. No one—and I mean, *no* one—wanted a former school shooter who had done time in prison to play the part of Jesus Christ. Besides, it was an event that no one had ever heard of and probably wouldn't care about.

"Are you sure it was me in your dreams?" If I asked her once, I asked her a dozen times. It just didn't make sense, but she repeatedly insisted that I was the one from her dream. I began digging deeper into this supposed dream, trying to find out when it had happened.

The dreams had started a little over two years earlier … at about the time I was being led out of Lake Braddock High School in handcuffs.

HIDING IN PLAIN LIGHT

Rita had no way of knowing what I had prayed for on the floor of my cell some seven months before. I had no way of knowing the radical way God had planned to not only answer my prayer but to do so much more than I had asked.

I think most people sometimes feel an unbelievable amount of pressure to make their lives work out for good. Work hard. Plan well. Try to mitigate risks and maximize opportunities. Avoid pitfalls, downfalls, and waterfalls. The hidden message we believe is that it's all up to us.

We may not want to admit it, but many Christ-followers feel this way as well, perhaps with a few adjustments. We can usually articulate that we know we can't get ourselves to Heaven. We admit *that* job is up to Jesus. However, we often live the rest of our lives leading up to Heaven as if it's mostly up to us. Therefore, if we make a mistake—in my case, going over a proverbial waterfall—we feel that we've blown it so badly that even God is like, "Look, you did this! Don't look at Me to fix it … I'll see you in Heaven, though."

The truth is that the God who is revealed in Scripture is limited by nothing, not even us. We can't throw anything at Him—not poor choices, screw-ups, or devastating face-plants—that removes His ability and willingness to intervene. I'm not saying we are not responsible for our own choices—just that God is not confined by them.

Moses murdering an Egyptian man (complete with the act of disposing of the body) somehow didn't stop God from making him into the deliverer. Jacob stealing his brother's iden-tity to run a con on his blind, dying father and take everything his brother stood to inherit somehow didn't stop God from making him the father of twelve sons whose names would become synonymous with the tribes of Israel (which was Jacob's new name, by the way). Jonah's completely rebellious refusal to do what God told him to do, coupled with his cruel bias against the people of Nineveh—evidenced by his great disap-pointment when they actually repented and didn't die in a fiery display of God's wrath—somehow didn't stop God from keep-ing him alive in a whale's belly and repeatedly pursuing him as he always seemed to run the opposite direction.

David's future adultery and murder, which God completely foreknew, didn't stop God from making him the king whose family line would later give birth to the Messiah. Hosea's wife's repeated return to promiscuity and prostitution didn't stop God from sending Hosea to redeem her. Peter's profanity-laden tirade denying that he even knew Jesus didn't stop God from using him to serve and sustain the early Church. And again, Saul's murderous rampage against Christians didn't stop God from changing his name to Paul and then making him the chief spokesperson for Christianity throughout the world.

God is not waiting for us to get to Heaven before He will become seriously involved in our lives, so we need not feel limited by our limitations. First Corinthians 2:9 (NLT) reminds us: "No eye has seen, no ear has heard, and no mind has imagined what God has prepared for those who love him." Ephesians 3:20 (ESV) echoes these sentiments by saying that God "… is able to do far more abundantly than all that we ask or think, according to the power at work within us …"

"Far more abundantly than all I could ask or even think" was exactly what was happening to me. It was so strange that, once again, I could tell God was up to something. I told Rita I would take the part on one condition: that she never tell anyone who I was. I was very specific. My name was to go in nothing—not in playbills, newspapers, or radio interviews. Nothing.

I actually had two reasons for hiding my identity. The obvious one was my own fear of being found out. However, I also knew that in a political town like DC, a story about a felon convicted for shooting up a school and who had recently been released early from prison playing the lead part of Jesus

Christ in the nation's capital would be a media powder keg that the slightest spark would set ablaze. You couldn't write this stuff—well, at least I was hoping no one would write this stuff.

Honestly, I didn't want the revelation of my past to destroy what she was trying to do. Rita's vision of what the play could be was so clear, and she had worked so long on getting it approved and in motion, that the last thing she needed was the lead character bringing it all down in flames.

Rita agreed to my terms, and in the years that would come, she never asked about my past. As far as I know, she never knew what I had done.

An Unexpected Cross To Bear

When I agreed to do the Passion play, I honestly didn't know what I was really getting into, but I was about to find out. This was not your run-of-the-mill, front-lawn-of-the-church, living-nativity-type production, not that there is anything at all wrong with those. This was a full-scale, fully cast, massive logistical undertaking. Stages and props were painstakingly constructed to accurately reflect what it might have looked like when, say, Pontius Pilate sheepishly pronounced condemnation upon Jesus and washed his hands before the crowd. From the Roman robes to the golden bowl (not solid gold, in our case), every detail was given meticulous attention.

In case you're unfamiliar with Passion plays or Easter pageants, "Passion" is the Christian term used to describe the events of the final week before Jesus's death, beginning with

His triumphal entry into Jerusalem and ending with His crucifixion and death on Good Friday. The word "passion" comes from the Latin word for "suffering," so directly stated, this event chronicles the ultimate suffering of Jesus.

Passion plays are not new, dating back mainly to Roman Catholic use in the Middle Ages, certainly as early as the Thirteenth Century, and quite possibly even earlier. Though the plays eventually died out, they were revived in the nineteenth century by both Catholic and Protestant churches and organizations. Oddly enough, they are widely considered to be secular events; that is, something the general public outside of church finds to be important and worthwhile. In fact, there are massive Passion plays performed regularly in hundreds of cities around the world.

The modern evangelical Christian probably doesn't realize this tradition is steeped in liturgy and history; I certainly did not. So, when I agreed to play the part of Jesus, I quickly felt the breadth of something larger than myself. I couldn't explain it, but in retrospect, I know that God was allowing me to literally have the most front-row seat possible to the reenactment of the most important moment in history and eternity. Beyond that, God was also connecting me with generations of Christians past and present, from a variety of traditions, languages, and ethnicities. Through this experience, I began to gain a perspective of Christ's immeasurable influence in this world, which is still merely a tiny taste of what is to come.

For a guy who had lived so long in isolation, this would prove to be an eye-opening change. Ironically, self-loathing and isolation can create the feeling that your viewpoint of the world is the most accurate one. It is not conscious, and it certainly doesn't make good sense, but it's true nonetheless. If my own thoughts are the predominant influence in my life, then I inherently trust these thoughts, even when they are telling me not to trust my thoughts. (You might want to read that again.)

Isolation is the kind of existence in which you have to continually deceive yourself unknowingly in order to continue living there. It's like living for years on end in an apartment that you hate and about which you complain daily. You can't stand it, or so you say, yet you keep living there. You like to talk about how expensive it would be to live elsewhere, but the truth is, you haven't really searched for other apartments. You just assume they're too expensive, and eventually, that assumption becomes belief. You believe you *must* live in your apartment when, in reality, you have options.

Either a simple Google search or time spent with other people who know the real estate market would reveal many other places to live that are comparable to your current accommodations, but you never look at them. While you continue to verbally declare your apartment to be the *worst*, you actually constantly declare your apartment to be the *best* by the sheer fact that you continue to live there, even though it would cost you nothing more to move.

This was me. I believed myself to be unworthy of love, even though I was still alive only because I was experiencing love. In isolation, this strange cycle of irrational thought begins to make sense. I didn't realize that I actually trusted in my own thoughts so much, but I did. God's answer was to keep putting people and experiences in my path that pushed me out of isolation and into the uncomfortable yet healing light.

This Passion play was going to be such an experience. I was going to meet people whom I would never have engaged on my own and who probably never would have engaged me. I was going to go places that I would have avoided and do things I would have loathed before. I was going to discover a hundred times over that my own thoughts about myself are not trustworthy—I needed others who would encourage, instruct, and continually point me back to my Source of hope.

Rusty was one such guy in my life during this time. He was one of the cast members from the play. As the props and equipment were all being purchased, designed, or constructed, Rusty and I were tasked with preparing the most important prop for the entire production: the cross.

My role was to carry the cross from the trial in Pontius Pilate's court set up on a stage in Lafayette Park all the way to the crucifixion on the steps of the Capitol. To be clear, that is about a two-mile walk, which takes most people around thirty-five minutes to make. I was going to do this walk while carrying a cross on my back, all the while being whipped, yelled at, and generally harassed by the Roman soldiers and the Jewish leaders. I may have been stout, but that would have been a bit too much to pull off while dragging a cross weighing in more than three hundred pounds.

That is why we built two crosses—one that I would carry down our own Washington DC version of the Via Dolorosa, and another on which I would hang at the Capitol Building. The cross I carried had an interior frame made of two-by-fours, just to help it hold its shape. It was then covered in Styrofoam that gave it the look of wood grain. The Styrofoam exterior was painted brown and *voila*! we had a cross that was lighter than the wood version but still substantial enough to require some effort to carry.

Since there were many points along the route where I was supposed to either be kicked or fall to the ground in exhaustion, a softer cross came in handy. This helped to limit how much damage or injury it might do if things stopped going according to plan and it accidentally fell on someone in the crowd or on a piece of property. (The last thing you really want is to crush a hotdog vendor's cart—along with his livelihood—with the cross of Jesus Christ.) It also meant that cross itself landed softer, which kept it from breaking apart after repeated drops.

I don't know who made the first cross, but I know who made the second: Rusty and me. We actually worked on it on the porch at Rita Warren's apartment in Arlington. It was quite the job because we used two huge logs from downed trees and carved them by hand into the respective crossbeams using hammers, chisels, and sanding tools. All told, it took us about a week to get it done. Of course, I was still teaching guitar during the day, so I could only work with Rusty during the evenings. For that week, I didn't take any shifts at TGI Fridays ... this just seemed so much more important.

Rusty and I developed a beautiful friendship. He played the part of one of the Roman soldiers. This meant that he had to treat me with disrespect and disdain when the play was going on; but when we were just being ourselves, he was just the opposite.

As we worked diligently on the cross and on other projects related to the play, he shared his life and his faith with me. He treated me with so much respect, taking an interest in my life. Having an older guy listen to me and care about me was just another one of God's invaluable blessings to me. I couldn't know the depths of my father wounds at that moment, but God knew, and he put guys like Rusty near me to show me what it meant to be affirmed and valued by other men instead of threatened, abused, and intimidated.

We worked tirelessly to carve that cross, shaping it into what it needed to be to accomplish its gruesome mission. Rusty not only shaped the cross, but he helped to shape my life. He mentored me during this time, teaching me what it meant to be a follower of Christ and also just to be a man of integrity. I think he knew that something significant and horrible had happened in my past, but it was obvious that I didn't want to talk about it, so he never pushed me to do so. He just loved me well.

When I think about the pain that so many people feel in this world today, especially teens and young adults, my heart longs for them to have a Rusty in their lives. We put bandages on wounds and casts on broken parts of our bodies for a reason: so that nothing or no one will touch them and make them hurt even worse. A good doctor or nurse won't just start jabbing medical instruments into a painful wound—they will help it heal by keeping it clean and protecting it from unwanted contact.

Rusty helped keep me clean. He also protected me by just being someone who cared and didn't require that I bare everything in my life. I just wasn't ready for that, and if he had pushed me, I might have bailed on the whole Passion play and who knows what else. He was patient. He was intentional. He was kind.

My hope is that as you read these words about my story, you will realize that you are someone's Rusty right now. They may be bristling with anger or on the verge of hurting themselves or others—and you may feel powerless to change them. The truth is: you are powerless to change anyone (that's Jesus's job), but you are not powerless—not in the least.

If you have any interaction with them at all, you have been afforded great power. You just have to recognize how to exercise it and how not to exercise it. Above all else, Rusty made it clear that I mattered to him, regardless of what I had struggled with. Yes, the things of my past needed to be discussed, and if I could have discussed them earlier with people I trusted, it would have probably helped me avoid a lot of excess pain in the years leading up to the writing of this book. But Rusty seemed to understand that you can't push a person to a place of honesty and vulnerability when they aren't yet willing to go … it has to be on their terms. You can, however, make it abundantly clear that you are open to listening if they ever want to talk.

I know the other way Rusty impacted me was by praying for me. Saying this almost seems cliché nowadays, which proves how little we actually expect God to listen and answer our prayers. Even people who claim Christianity as their faith tend to treat prayer as ritual to be done before a meal or at a church service, not an actual, relevant part of their daily lives in which they give God what they are facing and expect Him to act on their behalf.

People loved me well when they prayed for me consistently. Rita. Rusty. My mom. John Bonds. The trustees in prison. These are all people who supported me not just with kind words and kind actions (although those are important too) but with communication with the only One who could truly affect my life beyond behavioral modification. None of them could change my heart, but they knew the One who could.

Never underestimate the power of praying for someone whom you feel may be struggling or who is just "off" in some way. You may not know what is going on, but God certainly does, and He allows us to be involved by offering love and support in the supernatural realm when we talk to Him on their behalf. It's not that our prayers are necessary for God to care or to take action. Rather, He is inviting us into His own caring process already in motion as He takes action. After all, we can't even have a desire to pray for someone else unless God's Spirit is leading us to do so. It is not our prayers that are initiating the action; our prayers are simply an action that we've been invited to take within the ultimate action God is already taking.

The other thing about prayers is that they never expire. To us, a prayer prayed years ago is eventually forgotten, lost to the sands of time and our own limited minds. But God's mind is not limited, and He is not chafed by the sands of time as we are. What happened a few thousand years ago might as well have been yesterday to Him. Because He is outside of time, everything for Him is all in present, real time. This means that when we pray, He never forgets it, even when we do.

Not only that, but the emotions we felt at the moment we prayed—emotions that probably subsided or at least changed as time went by—are still completely fresh to God. So when you pray for someone in a moment but lose track of them in the future, never believe for a second that your prayer was wasted. God has their whole lifetime—and indeed, even eternity—to answer the heartfelt requests of anyone who calls upon Him.

Returning to James 5:16, we can really see how much prayer plays a part in the healing and growth we experience in relationships. I showed you how the first half of the verse demonstrates the way God uses honest, authentic community to continually heal our lives, which included both confession of wrongdoings and shortcomings. It is no accident that confession is supposed to be immediately followed by prayer. "Therefore, confess your sins to one another and *pray for one another*, that you may be healed" (emphasis mine). Part of the same verse reinforces why we should do these things in this order, namely because "The prayer of a righteous person has great power as it is working."

I didn't know at the time that I would be involved in this Passion play for a long time, not just the one year. It would take me places I never thought I would go, but it was friends like Rusty who most deeply affected me during the experience. He died of a heart attack about four years after the last Passion Play we did together, but his kindness, wisdom, and, indeed, his prayers continue to affect me today. I was once a shooter, but because of God's grace to not only rescue me but also to put people like him into my life, I have continued to be truly transformed into someone else altogether.

CHAPTER 9

Lifted Up

Extensive preparations were made for Good Friday, 1985. That was the day that would put Jesus in the middle of Washington, DC, the most powerful city in our nation and, quite possibly, the most powerful city in the world.

The props, wardrobe, makeup, and hair were second to none. Rita Warren had secured the costumes as a donation from a film company in Hollywood. Now a guy whose prison nickname had been "Hollywood" was wearing clothes created for a Hollywood set. The whole thing was surreal.

The actors came from all walks of life. There were doctors and lawyers; that is, people who spent their days in the professional arena making hundreds of thousands of dollars per year. They suited up right next to just plain, ordinary people who may not have been wealthy but who were just as valuable to the production. One actor owned a huge auto dealership near

DC while another was one of the team doctors for the Washington Redskins.

Then there was me: a former high school gunman. Of course, none of the other cast or crew members knew anything about my background at that time, and unless they have seen one of my stories on a few of the media outlets that have reported on me over the last few years, this book is probably the first time they will discover the truth about "the young man playing Jesus." That was what Rita always called me, and it was the only way she introduced me.

News outlets from all over the world set up shop and reported on the event as everything finally unfolded on that Good Friday afternoon in 1985. Rita had worked tirelessly for years to get this live Passion Play approved by both houses of Congress, so there was quite the buzz around town about it. She had done Easter pageants of sorts in the past but only with mannequins instead of live actors.

The play began in Lafayette Square just across from the White House. Just so you can understand the girth of this production, local law enforcement actually blocked off Pennsylvania Avenue. I stood on a large platform alongside the actor who played Pontius Pilate as well as the man who played Barabbas. Roman pillars towered near us on both ends of the platform.

As the actors in the crowd began chanting "Give us Barabbas!" I was suddenly taken aback not only by the fact that I was staring at the White House while thousands of people gazed upon me but also by the true story that we were depicting. Barabbas was a known criminal. An insurrectionist. A murderer. He was everything that normal people with children, families, and a desire for peace in their nation would seemingly not want out on the streets.

Yet the mob clamored for Barabbas, even as they demanded Jesus's death. What got me was that about two thousand years earlier, this moment on a platform actually took place with actual people. Barabbas was there, standing next to the Roman governor who was weighing his fate by the whims of a mob whose fire was being stoked by the religious leaders for their own selfish desires.

No doubt, Barabbas knew who Jesus was—he was the most famous person in all of Judea. This was the miracle worker who had healed thousands of blind people, deaf people, and people who couldn't walk. Even the demons listened and obeyed when He spoke, as did the waves of the sea and the wind. Thousands had sat on various hillsides feasting upon meals that Jesus multiplied with just a few loaves of bread and a couple of fish.

Only a few weeks before this moment in His story, Jesus had also been the dead raiser. The raising of Lazarus from the dead was the straw that broke the Pharisees' back, sending them into full-on scheming to put Him to death. I suppose the irony was lost on them—planning the death of the man who just raised a guy from the dead. Even so, Barabbas would have known all of this about Jesus, and now they were sharing a most unlikely stage as fellow criminals.

Except one of them had done nothing wrong, and both of them knew it.

Jesus also would have known who Barabbas was—and not just because he was omniscient. Barabbas couldn't escape his notoriety. And at this particular moment in his story, he probably knew the jig was up. He had skirted the edge of trouble one too many times, and now it was time to pay the price for his crimes.

It was a strange tradition that seems pretty odd to us in modern times. Imagine if the President of the United States were to release a hardened criminal every year based upon the direct vote of whatever people gathered outside the White House to clamor for their favorite criminal's release—and no other reason. Imagine that it really wasn't about their guilt or their innocence but was literally a straw poll based upon the whims of a mob in the moment. Yes, most presidents generally pardon many convicts, usually on their way out of office. But most of these are at least disputed cases, where there is reasonable doubt that the judicial system actually proved guilt beyond a reasonable doubt.

But not Barabbas. There was no doubt, reasonable or otherwise, about what he had done and what he deserved. Yet the people were asked to chime in on his fate—and they did. He was going to be set free while Jesus—the Messiah who had thrown the known world off its axis not just by His miracles but by His teachings and the kindness He showed to prostitutes and tax collectors—was going to be brutally murdered instead.

As I stood on that stage, I had the distinct feeling I was wearing the wrong costume. I had no business playing Jesus; I was the spitting image of Barabbas. I had acted murderously, even if, miraculously, no one was murdered. I was well known for my crimes. But just as Jesus traded places with Barabbas to take the cross, He had traded places with me too.

I was wearing His clothes and being seen not as myself but as Him. He was hiding me within His own identity. Later on, as I grew in my faith, I would come to know this is exactly what Scripture says Jesus does for us: "For you have died, and your life is hidden with Christ in God" (Colossians 3:3 ESV). I had once been dead inside, but when Christ pursued me, he put that death to death, bringing me to life. Now here I stood, hidden behind His image ... and just like Barabbas, I had been set free because He was willing to die in my place.

Of course, my depth of understanding was still so limited then. I felt the divine implications of playing Jesus instead of Barabbas, but it was more of a feeling than a full thought. Full thoughts have continued to come as the years have passed. I would say that I felt overwhelmed with a divine presence—a sense that God's own Holy Spirit was very near to me as I went through the various parts of portraying Jesus in all His suffering. I know that God used the role I was playing to keep bringing the realities of Christ's "big day"—the worst day of His life, but the best day of ours—to the world.

Many showed up for the purpose of seeing the play, but some others just happened upon it. In Washington, there is always something going on that involves large numbers of people descending upon the city. Besides Easter weekend, it was also time for the Annual Cherry Blossom Festival, so thousands of people from all around the world were visiting.

Security was high, and the logistics of blocking off roads and keeping the crowds at a safe distance from the actors was a logistical challenge. The local police were more than up to the task; after all, they were used to securing events with large numbers of people in attendance. The police made sure there were barricades, and they also rode motorcycles beside the procession.

Various actors filled the roles of the Romans soldiers, Mary Magdalene, Mary the mother of Jesus, the eleven disciples, and also just general townspeople who were walking with Jesus as I made the long trek towards the cross. I can only imagine what Rita was feeling at that moment. Her vision, right down to the young man who would play the part of Jesus, was being miraculously fulfilled before her very eyes.

As we approached the Capitol Building, I could see what seemed to be tens of thousands of people gathered along the processional route leading up to the Capitol steps. Many of them were tourists there to learn about our nation's capitol; little did they know that God had actually arranged for them an encounter with Jesus. Millions more watched on television, the exact number impossible to know. The BBC covered the event, which alone meant that it was aired to more than eight hundred million people around the world.

The prayer I had prayed in prison, asking God to show the world what He could do with my life, was constantly in my head. I even whispered it under my breath as I made my way toward the cross. To be clear, I didn't think for a moment that I was any kind of savior, and I wasn't just excited for the spotlight. The moment itself was a miracle to me—a tangible answer to my prayer.

But my fear remained, even as I felt such a profound sense of gratitude and awe at what God was doing in my life in that moment. As I walked up to the stage on the Capitol Building steps wearing a loincloth, a purple robe, and a crown of thorns, I was shaking because I still felt that someone was going to recognize me. I was wearing a wig that partially covered my face, which brought me a little comfort, but I always felt that it was only a matter of time before I would be found out.

The Roman soldiers laid me down on the wooden cross that Rusty and I had carved and constructed. The soldier in charge of hammering raised a huge, wide-head hammer high in the air and brought it down with great force on a piece of metal laying to the side, producing a loud clanging sound. I screamed out, heaving and writhing in fake pain, but thinking about the real pain Jesus felt when those nails actually pierced His wrists. For me, there were straps to hold onto as they raised me high into the air … Jesus had no such straps.

Max Lucado said it best: "He chose the nails."

Once I was raised up, I could see that some people in the huge crowed watching me were weeping because they were staring at the most compelling depiction of love this world has ever seen. They weren't seeing me; they were seeing an image of Christ laying down His life not just for the world at large but also specifically for them.

Seeing just an actor's rendition of the sacrifice Jesus made for us can help us realize a fraction of the love He must have for us. After all, as John 15:13 (ESV) reminds us, "Greater love has no one than this, that someone lay down his life for his friends." It is one thing to imagine what it means for someone to lay down his or her life, but it is another thing altogether to see it happening, even if only in a dramatic production.

Not that one must see a Passion play in order to understand the sacrifice Jesus made, but the actual, visual events that the people standing around Christ's actual cross witnessed with their own eyes were the very reasons that Jesus came. He came to be lifted up in that moment so that all could see His willingness to die and His eagerness to show the love of the Father.

This is why He didn't die in secret or just in front of his enemies. He died in Jerusalem during the Passover celebration. It was a time when thousands upon thousands of people would have made the pilgrimage to the city to observe the Passover. This was intentional for so many reasons, the chief being all of the prophecies and shadows of the Old Testament being fulfilled in Christ. The Passover was a time when the blood of a spotless lamb was offered as the symbol of life and protection for all who took refuge beneath it—and on this cross, this doorway between the perfection of Heaven and the fallenness of Earth, the blood of *the* Spotless Lamb would once and for all offer life and protection to all who took refuge beneath it.

Consider even the fact that God instructed Moses and the Israelites to eat unleavened bread during the Passover, mainly because they would not have the time to wait for the bread to rise before they would be freed from slavery in Egypt. In the Bible, leaven always symbolizes sin. So when Jesus called himself the Bread of Life, He was the unleavened bread of the Passover—the One without sin who would fill the hearts of all who are hungry for life, preparing them for their journey ahead.

There are many more connections between the Old Testament Passover and Jesus on the cross, but we mustn't miss the fact that His sacrifice was meant to be seen by as many people as possible. His visibility on Golgotha—with all the accompanying shame and despair of being in public eye—was a key element. It was a crucial reason that God took on a body to dwell among us. The Apostle John unpacks this important truth in John 3:14-15 (ESV): "And as Moses *lifted up* the serpent in the wilderness, so must the Son of Man *be lifted up*, that whoever believes in him may have eternal life" (emphasis mine).

This is another reference to Moses and the Israelites. Specifically, God allowed an infestation of poisonous snakes in their camp as punishment for their constant complaining and disbelief. The snakebites were fatal, though death was not immediate ... just like sin in our lives today. But God had mercy on them, even though they didn't deserve it. He told Moses to fashion a bronze snake and to put it on a pole so that everyone who would simply look up and behold this bronze snake would be healed from the poison.

When Jesus said He was going to be lifted up in the same way Moses lifted up the serpent in the desert, He was reinforcing the fact that His crucifixion is something to actually behold. This was not only true for those who were there at the actual event, but for everyone today.

A play is not necessary to behold the cross, though it may help. We should at least visualize the scene of Christ's crucifixion in our minds, giving it room in our imaginations. We should read the descriptions of it in the gospels, as well as other books. By doing this—by looking up at the One who was lifted up for our sins and for our healing—we can avoid inadvertently thinking of the crucifixion as merely a metaphor or a tall tale.

Secular historians agree that Christ was crucified, even though they may not agree about all the reasons why. If He really hung on that cross, then we should do our best to try to visualize what it must have really looked like—after all, everyone who "looks on Him" is granted rescue. I was experiencing the power of what happens when people look upon Jesus's sacrifice for them; I was just seeing it from Christ's perspective.

From my uplifted position, I could see the flashes of literally thousands of cameras. Obviously, there were no cell phone cameras back then, so these were flashes from the cameras of professional journalists as well as many tourists who had come to capture the beauty of all the monuments in and around the Washington Mall area but were actually encountering a sight they hadn't expected.

I was later told that the news coverage on that Easter weekend moved from images of Pope John Paul II performing sacred duties and ceremonies for Holy Week at the Vatican to me playing the part of Jesus Christ in Washington. But besides my mother, no one, not even the pope, knew who I was and what I had done only two years and four months earlier.

As I began to approach the death scene, my heart was almost bursting within me. I only had a few lines in the play and this was my biggest one. I was supposed to say, "My God! My God! Why have you forsaken me?" But instead, I said, "My God! My God! You are my king. You're the king of kings and the Lord of Lords!" *Oops*. I think that I was just so moved by God's love for me that I came out of character and said what I was thinking instead of what Christ said.

The good news is that I'm not sure anyone really noticed the change, or if they did, they never came to correct Jesus on what should have been His last words.

I did manage to correctly say my final lines: "It is finished! Into Your hands I commit My spirit!" Then I went limp on the cross. After a while, the Roman soldiers removed me and carried me off the set. There was a white van waiting for me behind the scenes and I was ushered away from the area.

That was Friday, but just like the actual events, Sunday was coming.

RESURRECTION DAY

After our Good Friday performance, I had a day to recuperate before the Easter Sunday Resurrection Service on the steps of the Capitol Building. It would again be in front of thousands of people and have major media coverage. And this time, I didn't have to walk for two miles carrying a cross to get there.

Before this event, we actually attended church near the White House as ourselves, not as characters. President Reagan attended the service. It was beyond surreal to sit in a room with the President and about four thousand other people when, only a few months earlier, I had been sitting alone in a prison cell. I sat next to Rita Warren and just took it all in, laying low and keeping my mouth shut.

After the service ended, I was ushered out of the sanctuary and into a room where I could change into my wardrobe.

We then walked through a set of private tunnels between the church and the Capitol. I would emerge near the steps where the Resurrection part of the Passion Play would be happening.

The event team had placed 144 lily plants, representing all the nations of the world, on the steps of the Capitol in the shape of a huge cross. It took up most of the space on the steps. When the time was right, I walked out from my hiding place dressed in a white robe and stood in the middle of this cross made from lilies.

To me, this moment was extra special for two distinct reasons. Obviously, the visual of Christ standing as the risen Savior among plants that represented the whole world was a powerful reminder of His love for all humankind and His desire that no one in this world should perish. But secondly, the fact that there were 144 lily plants reminded me that when I was at my lowest point, I thought I would be spending 144 years in prison. They were all seeing Jesus standing there, but the young man beneath the costume was thinking of where he *should be* at that moment: either rotting in a grave or rotting in a prison cell.

The real Jesus had kept both of those outcomes from happening.

Afterward, there was a reception inside the Capitol rotunda. Talk about *not* wanting to introduce myself to senators, members of Congress, and other dignitaries! For a former school shooter from several counties away in Virginia, that would be exposure on steroids. Luckily for me, I was the only one attending in character, so I didn't have to be anyone but Jesus to them.

I was taken to the top area overlooking the rotunda. There, one of the congressional officials stopped the reception and read an announcement: "Ladies and gentlemen, we have a special guest to introduce to you today."

He never actually said "Jesus Christ." He didn't have to. As I stepped forward into their view, the room erupted into applause and anyone sitting down stood up to give Jesus a standing ovation. I was blown away by the moment because I was literally witnessing a sea of great men and women—kings and queens of their own little parts of the world—standing and applauding Christ. It reminded me of the scripture that says every knee will someday bow and every tongue will someday confess that Jesus is Lord.

People from outside were also allowed to join the reception within the Capitol. I was taken from the upper area into the main room where everyone was gathered. I walked around with Rita as she introduced me as a distinguished guest to dignitaries, elected officials, and other influential people in politics and government. She kept her promise to me, never saying my name to anyone. She always just introduced me simply as "the young man playing Jesus."

I just smiled, shook hands, and sometimes touched people on their shoulders. There were many people there who were speaking other languages as well. I couldn't understand them, so I just touched their shoulders too as I circulated through the crowd. I just wanted to show them the love of Christ, even if I had no idea what they were saying. Besides, I knew that I had no business trying to speak words of wisdom, much less the words of Jesus.

The Hope Must Go On

The Passion play was a huge success. Rita Warren's dream had come true on so many levels. Even so, she wasn't done dreaming.

A few weeks after the event, she approached me with the idea of doing the same play in other major cities. Besides DC, we would go on to perform the Passion play in Boston, Connecticut, and New York City. To be honest, the first event had impacted me so deeply that I was a little disappointed it was over. So when she asked me, it didn't take long for me to answer yes. I loved the time we would spend together, if for nothing else than to hear her say "Buona Pasqua"—that is, "Happy Easter" in Italian.

I even promised I would get my lines right the next time I hung on the cross.

New York was our next destination. Washington, DC, is a major city with its own unique culture, but New York City is a whole other animal. This time, our *Via Dolorosa* would take us through the area near the Eleventh Police Precinct and conclude with the crucifixion in Times Square. The police precinct was a nasty, terrible place. It was a very old building that reeked of the humanity that was being processed and jailed there. There was urine on the floor. Here I was, back in a police station where people were being locked up for their crimes. In fact, my dressing room was a jail cell—you couldn't make this up if you tried.

But I wasn't wearing a jumpsuit this time. I was wearing a loincloth and a robe. As I sat there getting ready for my performance, a police officer walked up and said, "I need to make you aware of something. Before you go out here, you need to know that you could be killed. They don't like Jesus here. They might like him in Virginia or in DC, but people have a big problem with Jesus here in New York. Are you aware of this?"

I normally said nothing in these kinds of situations, and especially not to policemen. But in this case, I just nodded my head and said, "What better way to die than to die for my Lord?"

His expression revealed quite a bit of confusion. He paused for a second and said, "Okay, it's your tail. I just wanted to give you the heads up."

The thing was, I really meant it. I should already have been killed for the wrong things; though I wanted to live, if I were to be killed for the only thing that matters in this life, I was okay with it.

When we began our procession, the police worked hard to actively block off the streets and protect the actors, especially the Roman soldiers who created a perimeter around me, which meant they were the closest to the crowds. I have a very distinct memory of passing by many porn shops. Back then, there was no such thing as internet porn, so there were porn shops all up and down the streets. Men were lined up to go inside them.

I can only imagine what was going through their minds when they were waiting to enter a store that sold images of sex but instead an image of Jesus Christ dragging his own cross passed by them. At one point, I intentionally fell down in front of one of these shops because I felt a great deal of empathy for the guys standing there. It was not judgment; they were no worse than me. I knew what it was like to be enslaved to something that controls you in evil ways. I wanted them to see that a Savior saw them, yet was still willing to die for them, just as He had for me. As I lay there on the street, I looked up at them very slowly.

When they saw my eyes, they scattered in all directions. My prayer has always been that they didn't scatter away to be crushed by embarrassment or rebellion—I know that movie and how it ends. I hope that they were able to see Jesus and, just like the Israelites and myself, that seeing Him and the love He has for them would bring them healing from what was killing them.

There was another time that something incredible and unrehearsed happened during one of my falls in the middle of a dirty street. A black man came out of nowhere and somehow managed to get through security. He made a beeline towards me and honestly, if he'd had a knife or another weapon, he could have killed me before the officers could stop him.

But when he reached me, it became obvious that he meant me no harm. Quite the opposite, actually. He reached down and pulled the cross off my back. The security officers were still running toward us, but Rita yelled out, "Leave him alone! Let him carry the cross!" Just like another black man who carried Christ's real cross, Simon of Cyrene, my new friend carried my cross the rest of the way until we reached the area in Times Square where I was to be crucified. Tens of thousands of people witnessed this incredible moment, and I can only imagine how God used it to affect them.

Specifically in New York, I remember the policeman's warnings were legitimate. When I was hanging on the cross in Times

Square, the reactions were more colorful than when I did so on the steps of the US Capitol. People seemed to have mixed feelings. Some were moved to tears, some were apathetic, and some were downright hostile, to the point of cussing at me and even trying to spit on me. It was a little too close to the biblical narrative, if you ask me.

I think the image of Christ on the cross just hit them all in a raw place of emotion. The very topic of Jesus does this to people all the time. After all, I was once someone who spewed venom and hatred towards a cross that was shining light on me. But in this moment, I tried to stay focused, in a spiritual place. I wasn't there as an actor; I was there as a disciple who was showing people what my Savior was willing to do for them, even if they chose to spit on Him in return. I was a seed planter, not a fruit maker.

In Boston, the crucifixion occurred in the Boston Commons … and again it almost became a little too true to the original events. While I was hanging on the cross, a guy with a knife tried to run up behind me and stab me in the back. He had slipped in behind the crowd so he wouldn't be as easily seen. Thankfully, the police stopped him before he got to me. I never saw any of it, but I could hear a commotion behind me as they tackled and detained him.

If only he had known who he was actually trying to stab; that is, another criminal just like him. I don't know his name, but I know that he was taken to jail. I can only pray that his story from that point forward took a trajectory similar to mine.

All told, I played the part of Jesus for four consecutive years in four major metropolitan areas in the Northeast. Along the way, I saw a veritable host of different reactions to the image of Christ. But the image I had of myself still haunted me. No amount of makeup, memorized lines, or self-muzzling ever removed the shame.

Looking back, I know the whole experience was part of God's plan to keep showing me new depths of His love ... depths that should have drowned out my disgrace. Depths that should have forever quenched my need to make amends by trusting in the redemption that Christ had made for me on His cross. Literally, I was on that cross so many times, but I didn't get it then.

I realized how big of a deal it was. I saw the signs. I marveled at the grace. And I accepted it for my salvation. But I still struggled to accept it for my *transformation*—I just couldn't accept my new identity in Christ. I had seen the Passion, but I still felt that the suffering I deserved merited more back payment than the suffering Jesus had taken upon Himself on the cross.

And so, when the years of the Passion play ended, I began to drift. I didn't necessarily stop believing, but I definitely stopped fighting with my shame. I gave in to it and just began to live my life in more hiding, not sharing with anyone what had happened to me. I became exactly what many Christians are today: lukewarm.

And just as a glass of lukewarm water tends to turn your stomach, my lukewarm faith turned me towards places that would bring a lot of pain into my life, especially in relationships.

But the same God who reached His hand out to me in that school in 1982 wasn't about to stop reaching out to me over the years to come.

CHAPTER 10

Country and Blues

This next part of my story is tricky in places. Let me explain. There is a chance that some people will be angry that I'm telling my story. They might think that I should still be rotting in that prison cell ... at the least.

The fact that I would seem to have no business sharing hope with anyone is something that would be obvious to most people, including myself. However, the realization that I should share the hope of Christ as it is revealed in my story is itself a story that has been ongoing for over thirty-five years. We have already discussed the reasons why I think it is time to speak out, but in the pages we have remaining, I will also try to let you in on how I moved from a place of complete isolation to this place of being able to share.

Before we get there, though, I have to address the matter of my family. Today, I am married, and I have two children who are both grown. I also have grandchildren. I am about to share with you stories and details from years after the Passion Play up to now, but there are some parts of the story that I feel compelled either to keep purposely vague or to leave out altogether for their sake.

I have no qualms with dealing with the discomfort or danger that might come my way after my story is shared, but my family is another story. They weren't around when I chose to walk into that school, literally guns a-blazing. They didn't intentionally endanger so many innocent lives with their reckless cowardice. They didn't wrestle with and lose to the tormenting voices of death and destruction that I let into my head.

I did all of that, not them, so I have to be careful about the way I expose them to potential ridicule and even danger today. I put innocent people's lives in harm's way once before. I refuse to do it again.

I will never share their actual names or other sensitive information about them that could possibly reveal their identities. So when you hear me refer to them simply by "my wife," "my son," "my stepdaughter," or the like, it is not because I don't treasure them—I just feel compelled to protect them. The fact is their influence is pretty much immeasurable in my life. God has used the ups and downs of these most precious relationships to teach me, shape me, and help me grow.

Just to reinforce how real this situation is and its potential ramifications, we actually have an emergency protocol in our home for everyone's protection. We have set up ways that we do and don't answer the door, among other things. I know that almost everyone has security systems and emergency situational plans in place these days—it's just wise. We are no different in this way, but the truth is, my story is pretty different from most.

This means I will be sharing bits and pieces from many years and many relationships but not necessarily the whole picture of everything and everyone. I just wanted you to understand one of the reasons why.

Love Hurts

I can't look into your head and read your thoughts, but I bet you're wondering how a guy who has been rescued from so much in so many radical ways could ever possibly just start living the life of a nominal Christian. How does one go from death's door to two doors down from death row to literally watching from the cross as the world finds hope in the suffering of a Savior to marginally interested and mostly unengaged?

Talk about going from a hundred miles an hour to zero in a hurry.

The truth is, I don't think that most people who seem to grow weaker in faith do so through some grand, rebellious decision in a single moment of defiance. People drift. The winds of life and change and choices slowly blow into their sails while they are not really paying attention. Time passes, and when they look up, they are far, far away from where they were once anchored, but they never necessarily intended to drift there.

Once you find yourself drifting, it's all too easy to just continue doing so. The work required to admit that you have drifted, much less the work you think is required to row back toward the correct location, begins to feel ominous. Besides, who's to say that you won't just drift again?

This is less of a *mindset* and more a state of *mindlessness*. Regardless, I think drifting is what happened to me, even if it wasn't something I was actually thinking. It can happen to anyone, but there is a key element of the whole "drifting ship" metaphor to address as the largest cause: the anchor.

All boats that aren't tethered to an anchor or the shore will eventually drift. It is not a knock on any one boat in particular. Sailboats drift. Speedboats drift. Cruise ships drift. Kayaks drift. From fishing boats to canoes, an unanchored vessel will move with the currents and the winds. It is not about the boat at all; it is about the elements and the simple fact of whether any vessel of any size at any moment on any body of water is intentionally connected at all times to something stronger and more secure than itself. That's all that matters.

I wonder if you might see yourself or someone else you know in the ongoing details of my life. That's why I wrote this book: to let my difficult story be known by others who are facing their own difficulties. But it is all too easy to begin acting as if there is something significant causing the drift related to the specific person who is drifting, when in fact, all people drift if they are not anchored to something stronger than themselves. All people.

They may not all open fire in a school, but all people are prone to the winds and currents of this life … and all of them share an equal need to be anchored down by something. People of faith tend to be the worst at developing rating systems for brokenness. "Well, I may not be perfect, but at least I've never ..." (insert whatever they have never done).

If we're honest with ourselves, most of us have an "at least I've never ..." rating system inside us. *At least I've never stolen anything. At least I've never cheated on my spouse. At least I've never cheated on my taxes. Gotten a DUI. Been arrested. Had a hangover. Beat someone up. Hired a prostitute.*

We begin to think that the nature of our vessel—that is, our choices and experiences—dictates whether or not it matters that we have drifted. *My "sin" is merely schooner-sized, so sure, I may have drifted into silently hating my neighbor or someone of another race or perhaps living a life of bent truth that could never "technically" be considered lying, but at least I'm not like that guy.*

Take it from *that* guy—the guy who shot up a school: we all need grace.

Jesus actually dealt with the "at least I've never ..." attitude when he told the story of a Pharisee, which was someone characterized by many legitimate good deeds and a lot of piety, and a tax collector, someone who would have been known in Christ's day for consorting with the occupying enemy nation (the Romans) and for often cheating the common man out of extra money during tax season because there was nothing to stop him from doing so. Tax collectors were some of the most hated people among the Jews during this time because they padded their pockets at the expense of their fellow countrymen. It's no wonder Jesus was often criticized for hanging out with these guys ... you would probably have criticized Him as well.

Jesus tells the story in Luke 18:9–14 (ESV).

He also told this parable to some who trusted in themselves that they were righteous, and treated others with contempt: "Two men went up into the temple to pray, one a Pharisee and the other a tax collector. The Pharisee, standing by himself, prayed thus: 'God, I thank you that I am not like other men, extortioners, unjust, adulterers, or even like this tax collector. I fast twice a week; I give tithes of all that I get.' But the tax collector, standing far off, would not even lift up his eyes to heaven, but beat his breast, saying, 'God, be merciful to me, a sinner!' I tell you, this man went down to his house justified, rather than the other. For everyone who exalts himself will be humbled, but the one who humbles himself will be exalted.'"

You don't necessarily have to be a Pharisee to do what this Pharisee did—rate your own level of offense against someone else's. I'm not saying, as many people claim the Bible says, that "all sins are the same." The Bible absolutely never says that. Different actions taken most certainly bring about different levels of consequences in this world. My story reveals this to be not only true but also just common sense. What I did deserved prison, if not death.

What the Bible does indicate throughout the gospels is that all sins make us equally in need of God's forgiveness and grace. Romans 3:23 (ESV)—"... for all have sinned and fall short of the glory of God"—is a clear statement that we all equally need God's unmerited favor and mercy, even if we haven't all committed what we would consider to be some "heinous" act against society.

We often use the term "Pharisee" in a derogatory way—it is not usually a compliment. But the truth is, if there was a different label for the same kind of person in our modern age, odds are you would like them. They would be the neighbor with the tidy yard, a seat on the council of your subdivision's HOA, someone who was always willing to loan you their garden tools when you needed them. We think of Pharisees as "bad guys" who were actually doing despicable things behind the scenes (and some of them were), but most of them were the epitome of good neighbors—the ones you would ask to keep watch over your home while you go on vacation just in case any "questionable" characters come snooping about. To be clear, you would not think of Pharisees as the "questionable characters."

This is proven by the impressive list of things the Pharisee in Jesus's parable prays about—and let's not gloss over the fact that he is actually going to church (in his case, a Jewish synagogue) and is actually praying, something a lot of people never do. He was also someone who exercised extreme self-discipline through the act of fasting twice a week (how many of us pull that off?) and who was extremely generous in donating money to good causes. Put it this way: if your kid was going to all the neighbors asking them to contribute to a school fundraiser, you would have no issue letting your child ring this guy's doorbell.

Jesus is not saying the Pharisee is "bad" in the sense that we think of the word. He clearly lives a disciplined, productive life and honors God with his church attendance, prayers, and giving. Jesus is saying that the real issue is this: does he trust in *these* things as the basis for his justification before God?

In other words, does he think he doesn't really need the free gift that God offers to everyone through the death, burial, and resurrection of Christ because he is doing just fine on his own?

All offenses are not the same, but the greatest offense is found in the darkest recesses of the heart—and all of us have those areas. That is what Jesus was saying—that no amount of do-gooding, civic responsibility, guilt tripping, or good intentions can truly change the heart. Only grace can do that. Otherwise, we all drift, no matter how clean, dirty, cheap, expensive, big, or small our ships may be.

We all need the anchor of grace, and *that* is what Christ came to offer. He offers not just behavioral modification but a heart exchange for all those—Pharisee and tax collector alike—who will admit that, regardless of our track record, our hearts are sick and need healing. It is a gift that no one can be good enough to earn, and in fact, the only deterrent to receiving it is thinking that you are already good enough without it. But to all who admit their inability to change their own hearts, the gift is free. This is strange to Pharisees, especially when they see tax collectors getting off seemingly scot-free.

Isn't it funny how most people think that God cares about their church attendance, giving, and fasting—the good behavior—more than anything else? This is actually the exact opposite of what Jesus came to reveal. He didn't come to let sinners off scot-free; he came to pay their debt, which is what really offends the Pharisees. He didn't change the payment system for their offenses; rather, He paid off what we all owe at the highest interest rate possible. I may not have actually felt the nails, but as a guy who carried a cross and felt the eyes of the world looking upon me, I can only imagine the high price He paid.

He basically took out "a hit" on Himself. He walked himself out to the docks, let his greatest enemy put His feet into the hardened concrete, and then willingly took a "swim with the fishes." He drowned in our sins so that we might have the opportunity to be lifted from the dark depths and breathe new life. He sank to the lowest depths, but he did not stay there. However, he did become the weighty, dependable anchor of the soul for anyone who is willing to accept His free gift. It can't be earned but only requires the acknowledgement that we all drift.

Or as a Pharisee-turned-pastor who was once named Saul but later Paul put it, all have sinned. All have offended. But all have access to rescue. The only condition to be saved from drowning is admitting that you're drowning. So if you know someone who is in trouble, perhaps in your own family or community—someone of the "tax collector" or "school shooter" variety, perhaps—I pray that you will be able to show empathy towards them—not because their *crimes against humanity* aren't greater but because each of our *crimes against divinity* are equal.

WANDERING

Why did I drift away from the anchor of a strong faith in Christ? Above all, it was simply a choice—or better said, a series of choices—that I made. No one else was responsible for them.

As much as I do not blame or hold my stepdad responsible for my actions at Lake Braddock High School, I want to make it crystal clear that I do not blame or hold anyone else liable for the decisions I made about the season of my faith.

That being said, while I carry the weight of responsibility, there were certainly circumstances that influenced my decisions. None of us can live our lives independent of others. People affect us in a million different ways, both positively and negatively. No person is truly an island, even if they truly want to be. Just as we can't avoid sharing the air with the people around us, we can't avoid sharing life either.

The beginning of my drift away from Christ began occurring because of a woman I became interested in. The bottom line was that I was lonely and wanted to be loved, plus there was the matter of sexual attraction. The shame that I still carried was a heavy weight, so it seemed easier just to do something that would seemingly keep it out of sight; that is, disappear into a new life with someone who I thought would love me.

Since I don't want to reveal many details that affect other people in my family's past, present, or future, suffice to say I met the girl in Virginia while I was teaching guitar to the kids and doing the Passion plays. When the program ran out, I actually reconnected with my real dad and began working as a plumber for a company in Winchester. My uncle owned it, and many of my cousins and other family members worked in that industry.

The girl and I married in 1987. Ours was not a godly marriage. I married her for all the wrong reasons, mainly physical attraction, lust, and the deep, deep desire to not be alone. We had two beautiful children pretty early on. I worked fifteen-hour days to give her and the kids the best I had to offer. In fact, for the sake of my family, I even tried attending a small church down the street from our house, just hoping it might help heal the issues in our marriage and family that seemed to be there from the very beginning.

Unfortunately, she had a drug problem that just kept getting worse. We started off in a lot of other unhealthy patterns that only worsened as the years began to pass. The relationship began with a lot of passion and not much of anything else, so once those emotions began to cool amid the ups and downs of daily married life, it morphed into a lot of fighting, especially as her drug use continued to worsen. Even though we had two amazing children, it became apparent that we just couldn't work it out.

Mistakes were made on both sides, and regardless of who was more at fault, our relationship ended in divorce in 1995. The divorce made me bitter, mainly because of the custody battles that followed. I fought hard to keep my kids and also to keep them out of the world of drugs that their mother was living in. But once again, it felt like I couldn't quite escape my past. Her attorney used my history in the courtroom, and I lost my kids, which caused me to drift even further away from God. It hurt so much.

Before we were divorced, my wife had been unfaithful, turning to another man whom she would quickly marry and also divorce. Today, she resides in the state women's prison as a result of her many drug charges over the years, I still pray she finds the love of Christ in her life because He loves her the same as He loves me, even in our sin. He continues to reveal Himself to us all.

I can see His love clearly now, but in those moments of my failed marriage and separation from my kids, it was pretty foggy. I decided it was time to get away from Winchester and pursue other dreams. I knew it would take a lot of effort to continue to regularly see my kids, which was a non-negotiable even though they now lived with their mother and her new man. Even so, I decided to get a new start by making a big move to Nashville, Tennessee, in 1996.

Music City, USA, was the place to be in the 1990s if you wanted to pursue fame and fortune in songwriting or as an artist in the country music industry. I decided to pursue both. My guitar playing was above average, and I had a pretty good voice.

I had begun singing and writing songs back in Virginia, giving shows for various events like the Apple Blossom Festival in Winchester. Most of the shows I played were local events or fundraisers for organizations like the Red Cross. I was writing my own tunes as an amateur songwriter, but I also performed a lot of cover songs from other artists. The truth was, I could pull off a dead ringer of Elvis, which would play into my career later.

I had laid down some tracks a few times in local recording studios in Winchester, but most of my music career up to that point involved playing covers wherever I could land a gig. Of course, I wasn't about to go by the name of Jamie Stevens, a name that would have still been pretty easily recognized in Virginia for something more than my music career—something also a lot less desirous.

By the time I moved to Nashville, I was already going by the name Jimmy James. Eventually, I changed it again to James Richards and finally to TJ Stevens ... anything not to be associated with Jamie Stevens, the guy who was once a shooter in Virginia. It was a new start for me, so a new name seemed to fit the bill.

I moved into the Rock Harbor Apartments on the Northwest side of Nashville. I was able to get a job with a local plumbing company making decent money. Believe it or not, my work in the plumbing industry around Nashville was one of the ways I made some pretty major connections in the music industry. All told, I ended up working for three different companies, and one of them found me regularly servicing a house in Goodlettsville ... the home of one Garth Brooks.

One time, a pipe burst in one of the smaller houses on Garth's property that he used as a studio. I was digging out the pipe by hand out in the cold when Garth walked up to check on me. I always called him "Mr. Brooks," and I never told him I was a songwriter or interested in the music industry. He was very worried that I was working out in the cold in a T-shirt, so he went to his pickup truck and brought me a jacket. It was one of the jackets made for his most recent tour. He threw it down to me in the muddy hole, and I expressed my gratitude.

A few hours later, he came back by to check on me again and found me still in the hole but not wearing the jacket. "Why are you not wearing the jacket?" he asked.

"Mr. Brooks, that jacket is way too nice to get all messed up in this mud."

He smiled, walked to his truck, and brought back a second jacket that was identical to the first, throwing it to me as he had the first time. "Here, now you can work in this one and keep the other one for later." His down-to-earth kindness to a simple plumber like me affected me deeply.

Other people affected me during that time as well. The owner of one of the plumbing companies used to try to speak into my life—not really in the area of faith but more so with my life choices and whatnot. Once when I was complaining about my circumstances, he "encouraged" me to get busy making changes and taking ownership of my life. Well, that's what he meant. What he actually *said* was something like, "Your life sucks because you suck."

It may not have sounded like very sage advice at the time, but I knew what he meant, and it actually helped me remember that, for the most part, life wasn't just randomly happening to me. Sure, there were circumstances beyond my control, but I was the main variable in all my problems … and most of the time, my choices not only contributed to but actually caused my issues. I needed to avoid self-pity and take ownership again.

I wasn't there yet, but God was not done pursuing me. I may have been my biggest variable, but His undeserved grace was still my constant.

I actually enjoyed plumbing work, but I really struggled with the rules and expectations of some of the companies I worked for. One of my bosses required that all of us workers gross at least a thousand dollars every day on the job; that is, if we wanted to keep our jobs. This meant that I often had to charge three hundred dollars to fix a simple flapper or a leaky valve. They call it "piece work." Besides this, trip charges were at least seventy-five dollars.

I just couldn't stomach it any longer—walking into some old lady's house who was obviously on Social Security and charging over three hundred dollars to replace a twenty-dollar supply line. I eventually quit and moved to the other side of Nashville into the Inglewood neighborhood near Gallatin Road.

While I was trying to get any gigs I could writing or singing, I did what most aspiring artists in Nashville do: I got another job or two. I ended up working at a nightclub downtown on Second Avenue called Graham Central Station, as well as another club called Denim & Diamonds on Gallatin Road. I was a cook, a maintenance tech, and at times, a bouncer—a real renaissance man.

The most significant thing that happened to me there was meeting another girl. She was an extremely attractive ventriloquist. At first, I remained mostly disinterested toward her because I was too busy working so I could keep sending child support back to Virginia while also trying to make it in the music industry. Even so, she kept pursuing me, and I was taken aback at how good she was to me.

She eventually gave me her number, but I never called. We lost touch for about a month or so but then ran into each other at the club one evening. I finally asked her out on a real date. It felt nice to be wanted and pursued by someone. Once we started dating, things took off pretty quickly. Too quickly.

One thing led to another, and we were married in a matter of months. We never had any kids of our own, but she already had two kids from a previous marriage, a boy and a girl about seven and nine years old respectively. Those kids were probably the best thing that ever happened to me in Nashville because they helped me deal with the fact that I was not seeing my own kids very often. I would drive back to Virginia or sometimes fly my kids out to Nashville to see them for visitation, but the expense and distance made seeing them a difficult endeavor. I always tried to check up on them, always paid their child support, and always let them know how much I loved them.

Divorce sucks.

My Nashville Experience

A lot of people in this country probably don't understand exactly what kind of town Nashville is. It is every bit as much of an entertainment hub for writers, artists, and industry executives as Los Angeles or New York, especially in the realm of country music.

It is a town of hustle, meaning that anyone who wants to try their hand at "making it" in the music business has to be willing to work hard today and even harder tomorrow. It is also a town of relationships. Sure, you generally have to have talent to make it, but incredible talent overflows among people in Nashville, from college kids to homeless people, from struggling waitresses to rich housewives, from sweaty landscapers to simple plumbers.

Everybody in that town has a guitar and a dream, so what really counts the most is *who* you know.

I became connected with a lady named Pat Harris who took an interest in me as a songwriter. She was well connected in Nashville and took me to a lot of songwriter events where I was introduced to various producers, writers, agents, and influencers in the industry. As a writer, I ended up working with EMI as well as Curb Records—again, mainly because I knew people who worked there.

One of the craziest things that ever happened to me in Nashville had to do with the movie *Hope Floats*, which featured Garth Brooks's cover of the Bob Dylan song "To Make You Feel My Love." I was downtown at the famous Wildhorse Saloon when the manager began asking if anyone could sing this song. It's Nashville, so of course, two or three people walked up to her and said they could do it. I was one of them.

She took us to the area by the back staircase, pulled out a guitar, and said, "Here, play it." The other two people played it first, but I could tell they didn't really know the right chords or the feel of the song. Then I played it, and I guess it went pretty well because the manager looked at me and said, "Okay, you're up in ten minutes." That night, I played a Garth Brooks cover at the Wildhorse—not even knowing I was going to perform it when I left the house earlier that evening.

Another time, I went to the Nashville Songwriters Association International (NSAI) convention. There were a lot of bigtime songwriters there, as well as artists and agents. When they drew ten names randomly out of a hat and let those ten people compete with their best songs, my name was among them. Even more shocking than that, mine was one of the top two winning songs chosen. I couldn't believe it! The winners were given backstage passes to the Grand Ole

Opry as well as an opportunity to play at the Roy Acuff Theater in Opryland, which was a pretty big deal at the time.

The song I had written was called "Little Things In Mind."
It was a half-religious, half-love song that turned a few heads.
I actually ended up signing a deal with ASCAP and found
myself in the writing rooms upstairs in the ASCAP building
on Seventeenth Avenue. At first, I thought I was a big deal,
but when you write with "real" songwriters, they put you
in your place pretty quickly.

I also used to sit near the BMI building behind Shoney's right
off of Demonbreun Street, set up a little amp, and play covers
and new songs I was working on. I could make about eighty
bucks a day from people giving me tips as they walked by.
I learned a lot about myself and about the songwriting industry
from those experiences.

I finally got a chance to sing for tourists from all over the
country at the LeGarde Twins theatre club on Music Row after
the owner noticed me on the street and liked my music. One
Friday night, I performed my typical ending to my set: an Elvis
medley. Immediately afterward, a fairly young guy approached
me and said, "How would you like to meet the guy who played
on all of Elvis's songs?"

I looked at him like he was some sort of wacko until he said
the name: "Hank Garland." That name stopped me in my tracks.

"Isn't he dead?" I asked suspiciously.

"No," the man replied, "he's alive and well … and is across
the street in a hotel."

Hank Garland was one of the most influential musicians
who ever played in Nashville back in the fifties and sixties.

He played many of the guitar tracks on Elvis's hit records. He had also worked with legends such as Patsy Cline, Mel Tillis, Marty Robbins, Roy Orbison, Conway Twitty, and Boots Randolph. It was too much of a crazy possibility to say no, so I agreed to go with him. I did pull the owner of the club aside and said, "Listen, if I don't come back in about two hours, call the police."

The young guy took me across the street to a hotel room. When he opened the door, a big, burly guy yelled, "I told you not to bring anybody over here!"

"Dad," the young man replied, "This is TJ Stevens. You gotta hear what he sounds like when he sings."

"Dad" protested a few more times but then finally invited me in. I couldn't believe my eyes: there were antique, pristine, priceless guitars lined up from one side of the room to the other. There was also a bigtime producer named Bucky Barrett sitting right there next to the real Hank Garland.

The old, burly guy was Billy, Hank's brother. The young guy who brought me there was Brian, Billy's son and Hank's nephew. My mouth was hitting the floor. I was standing near a legend, and I had no idea what to do. Hank looked at me and finally said, "Well, go ahead."

I guess that was the magic cue. Hank grabbed one of the guitars and said, "What do you want to do?"

"How about 'Are You Lonesome Tonight'?"

He nodded and began playing chords I had never seen or heard before. Then it hit me: it sounded exactly like Elvis's record. I still get goose bumps thinking about it. I began singing as he played. He stopped about halfway through the song and said, "Wow. No one's ever sang that song with me but Elvis Presley. Good job."

To make a long story short, that experience sparked a long friendship with Hank, Billy, and Brian. At their request, I ended up performing at the Park Vista Hotel a few months later for the American Country Music Award Show where Hank was receiving some sort of legendary award. Our friendship led to me performing in a lot of different venues. But Hank mostly liked to hear me sing Elvis tunes—no monkey suit or other imitation antics ... just the voice.

I worked hard to make my way as a songwriter. My biggest song was probably "Unknown Soldier," which was specifically written for military families. It was featured on WSMV Channel 4 on a show called *Unsung Heroes*. I was still afraid that someone would notice who I really was when my face flashed across the television.

I went on to do a live morning-show interview with deejay Jeff Lyons on WKDF radio. It was a surreal moment when he played the tune on the air and calls began streaming in. I received hundreds of messages from military families all across the country thanking me for the song. And since WKDF was playing it, Jim Carter, president of the Country Music Association (CMA), reached out to congratulate me and talk about it. We had a great conversation, and he gave me some solid advice about the business of music production. As a songwriter, just to get a call from him was huge.

After that, I was booked at the request of the Ed Rufo, founder of Operation Eagle's Nest and Chairman of the Middle Tennessee Better Business Bureau. He invited me to perform my song for the soldiers of the 101ˢᵗ Airborne at Fort Campbell, just across the Kentucky state line. I opened for country artists Jessica Andrews and Eric Heatherly. I was also asked to sing at the officers' military ball, which was an honor.

Within every CD case, we packed an envelope addressed to Operations Eagle's Nest so people could send money to help the families of soldiers deployed during the war in Iraq. After all my CDs sold out, I never printed more because I worried that too much exposure might lead to my past also being exposed. I had found purpose in helping others, even though I knew that if they were to find out who I really was, every one of these new and exciting doors would close.

The experiences I had with those heroes affected me so deeply, to the point that dormant elements of my faith were being stirred. I wanted to be known as a "somebody," which was true of almost everyone in Nashville, but for me, it was deeper. I was running from my past identity, trying unsuccessfully to bury my head in the sands of fame and notoriety. I learned so much that would help me later in my life, but during that season, I wasn't just chasing a dream; unfortunately, I was running from God as well.

Even so, God kept putting opportunities in my path that reminded me of His higher purposes—like helping the soldiers—whispering to my wayward heart that there was more to real life than just fortune or fame.

CHAPTER 11

The Winding Path Back Home

Looking back, it is so obvious that God wasn't done pursuing me, even as I remained mostly ambivalent toward Him. Besides the sense of purpose I found in helping soldiers' families, other snippets of the light that I used to walk in would resurface every now and again. I couldn't see them clearly from where I was at the time, but now I can see they were all around me. I guess the important things in life are sometimes harder to see up close.

For example, when I used to hang out near Music Row singing for tips from tourists and passersby, I met a homeless man who lived behind the dumpster at the back of the Shoney's restaurant parking lot off of Demonbreun Street.

Every day that I would sing, he would come and listen to me. We became friends. Even though I was in a season of life when I was mostly looking out only for myself, I felt compassion for the guy.

So one day, I took him into the Shoney's for a meal. No doubt, the manager knew exactly who he was because when he saw him, he tried to throw him out. "No, he's with me," I insisted. We sat and he ate a real meal like a real person. After I paid, I decided to take him somewhere very special to Nashvillians: Opryland USA.

Today, Opryland is mostly known for the enormous Gaylord Opryland Hotel, the Grand Ole Opry, and the adjacent Opry Mills mall. But back in those days, a huge theme park was located where the mall is today. It was a preferred destination for hundreds of thousands of thrill seekers and music lovers from all over the country. Rollers coasters and theaters covered the park, which was laid out in various musical genre themes.

I knew that others would look down on my friend because of his appearance, so I took him to my apartment to let him get cleaned up. I also gave him some of my clean clothes. While he was changing, I noticed that his leg had a horribly infected wound. It looked painful, but he didn't complain.

Of course, walking through an amusement park would have been way too much for him to physically endure, so I secured a wheelchair for him. I pushed that guy all over Opryland. I saw a completely different man than I had known up that point—he was smiling, laughing, and having the time of his life. I think that for that one day, the guy felt human again.

He thanked me over and over again, but honestly, I think I received more from the experience than he did. Sadly, I found out not too long after our little day trip that he had passed away behind that dumpster near Music Row. I think the experience caused me to recognize just a sliver of the light I was running from … it wasn't enough to pull me out of my hiding, but it was there, and it wasn't going away.

The other thing that jumps out to me during that season was the way my heart was moved to defend battered women. Nashville was a growing, bustling metropolitan area with quite the crime rate and quite the nightlife—and I was living right in the middle of that nightlife. I have come to conclude that very few good things happen at 2 a.m. in a downtown area, especially when people have been drinking a lot.

On multiple occasions, I saw men mistreating women on the side of the road. Sometimes, these were situations with prostitutes and their pimps, but that didn't matter to me. I had seen my mom beaten too many times—and I was no longer that scared little boy.

This meant that my first inclination was to jump in and rescue the women being hurt. Sometimes it helped, but sometimes, it caused the woman to beg me not to hurt the guy who was hurting her. To this day, any woman who is caught in such a situation, by choice or otherwise, just breaks my heart. My mom once felt trapped and unable to stop the pattern of abuse in her life, so I hate to think that any woman out there might feel trapped in the same cycle of hopelessness.

One time in particular, I was driving on the interstate at about 3 a.m. with my friend, Brian Garland, who was visiting

Nashville to see me. Brian had become much more than just a friend; he was truly like a brother to me. When we got together, we had a lot of fun, and both of us could get a little cocky, mostly in good fun. (I remember one such young man who used to attack the biggest guy in the prison just to prove a point.) I think he mostly just liked the fact that using his uncle's name, Hank Garland, helped him get into some clubs around the city, mostly the places where I was regularly playing.

I was actually trying to get him to tone down his macho bravado a bit when we saw a woman who was running away from a van on the side of the highway—then I was pretty glad he was feeling so confident because we might need a little strength. She waved us down, so we pulled over and she ran towards us with a panicked look on her face. She slammed her hands on the hood screaming, "Please help me! He's trying to kill me!"

I yelled at Brian to tell her to get into the car—quick! She climbed into the back seat, slammed the door, and we hightailed it out of there. The guy in the van had been trying to assault her. As we drove away, it became apparent that she was a prostitute. I felt a twinge of both compassion and pseudo self-righteousness, which is a weird combination. "I think somebody is trying to tell you something," I said to her in a solemn tone. I was so oblivious to the fact that I was running from God and had once hit rock bottom the same way that any person could. The truth was, Someone was also trying to tell *me* something; I just wasn't ready to listen.

"I'm just so glad you showed up when you did," she replied. I think that events like the one she had just escaped from were pretty normal for her. This affected me deeply, but there was seemingly nothing I could do about it. And above all, I was in no place to talk to her about "whomever" it was who was "trying to tell her something." She asked us to take her to a phone booth, and after she made a call, someone came to pick her up pretty quickly. I remember telling Brian that God had put us in the right place at the right time to help that poor soul and that I hoped she would be able to get out of that situation. Then we called it a night and never shared what happened that evening with anyone.

A Bible, an Old Man, and a Daughter's Request

I was living the fast-paced life of an aspiring musician in Nashville, one that many people around the city know very well. I was chasing after everything that promised to bring me fulfillment, and while I was having some fun, I still felt very, very empty. I had memories of my time among people of faith who had loved me well, never judging me and always accepting me, even when I asked them to never tell anyone my name. It was as if they didn't care what I had done—as if they valued me just for the human being I was.

I had a lot of friends in Nashville, but in my heart of hearts, I knew that if any of them ever found out I was once a school shooter, they would reject me so fast it would make my head spin—not to mention what the industry's reaction would be. I would basically be nuclear. Untouchable. No matter how much we drank together, sang together, or recorded together, I was beginning to feel that it was all based on a lie … on a literal false identity and a fake (or at least concealed) backstory.

The only time I had ever felt truly accepted and loved (outside of my mom) was when I was seeking Christ and living life with His people—with the trustees in prison, the young adults from the youth group, and the actors and crew from the Passion plays. I found myself strangely being drawn back to that life, even though I knew I had become the ultimate hypocrite.

Regardless, I actually found myself walking into a church near Opryland: Two Rivers Baptist. I don't remember what I told my wife at the time, but I made up some story about where I was going because she would not have been okay with me having anything to do with church or God. She would have cussed me out for going. She was into Wicca and the occult.

I snuck into the back of the church as discreetly as possible, inconspicuously snagging a back seat. I just wanted to be near something related to God, if only for a few moments in secret. I was hoping no one would even notice I was there … but someone did. A man walked up to me out of the blue and said, "I don't know who you are. I don't know where you're from. But God told me to give you this Bible, so I want you to have this."

If deer in headlights look surprised, I must have looked like a deer staring straight into the sun. "Really?" was all I could muster.

"Yeah."

I took the Bible from him and he walked away. I don't remember what the pastor said that day in the service, but that

Bible has never left my side. I took it home and hid it, of course, but I never forgot that moment.

This experience was a key part of helping me at least begin to see the world of Christianity—and specifically, the Church—through different lenses. Again, most of my exposure to Christians had been outside of the Church. I had really come to a place where I looked down pretty harshly on "church people," expecting them to be narrow-minded, judgmental, and too heavenly minded for any earthly good. After this experience, I did not begin attending church, but seeds were growing within my heart.

One of the other main factors that began drawing me back to God came in a very unsuspecting package. We were living in Goodlettsville at the time. There was an old man who drove an old pickup truck who came by our house every Thursday for no other reason except to remind my stepdaughter that the bus heading to church would be by on Sunday to pick her up. She had made some really great friends at a local church—and this old man just wanted to make sure she was still planning on coming every Sunday.

Her mother was *none* too happy about it, but you try telling a preteen girl that she can't hang out with her friends. I was still very cynical myself, so it was easy to play the part and talk about all the church people she was interacting with as if they were a bunch of hypocritical losers. I didn't let on that my heart was unsettled.

I dreaded seeing the man's old Datsun B210 truck pulling up in the driveway. He would take forever to make his way up to the door. When he would knock, I would always try to avoid answering the door. I would send my stepdaughter to handle him. He had to be in his mid- to late eighties, but he didn't let age stop him from being faithful to remind our ten-year-old daughter that she was very valued in their community. I think it meant a lot to her.

Eventually, I got up the nerve to answer the door every once in a while. We would exchange niceties, but above all, he would tell me how much the people at the church loved my stepdaughter. I would tell him that she really enjoyed the Sunday School. That was about the extent of our interaction.

This went on for about two years. Finally, when he knocked one night, I answered the door and came out onto the porch with him. "Can I talk to you for a minute?" I asked.

"Sure!" he kindly replied.

"Not here," I whispered. "Can we go to your truck?"

With a strange expression on his face, he nodded in agreement. Once we were inside his cab, I said, "Would you pray for me?" I went on to tell him about the life I was living—the lifestyle of hopping around clubs, doing shows, and living in a marriage that I knew wasn't healthy.

He looked at me with intense compassion, something I hadn't seen in anyone's eyes since the days I had hung out with ladies like Rita and carved out crosses with guys like Rusty. "I'd be glad to pray for you right now," he gently said.

I freaked out in a low whisper. "No! Don't do it here. Do it ... do it somewhere else."

Our conversation ended as quickly as it had begun, but the next Thursday, he came back again. When I opened the door, he looked around to make sure no one was listening and quietly said, "Hey, man, I prayed for you."

"I appreciate that," I replied. "You just don't know what that means to me to have somebody speaking to The Man Upstairs on my behalf."

"I'm going to pray for you every week," he said. And he did.

But one day, he didn't show up. My heartbroken stepdaughter was the one who told me about his death, calling him by his name. To this day, I don't remember his name, but I know that I will see that guy again someday in Heaven … and when I do, I will never forget his name again, nor his willingness to drive up the driveway of a rude man like me, to listen to my weird requests, and to keep praying for me. I truly believe he was just another one of those people God placed in my life for the exact moment I was living.

Next time you feel that you're not getting through to someone, I hope you will remember the old man who refused to forget me, even when I treated him poorly. Since prayers never expire, the old man's prayers joined with the prayers of my mother, my friends from the play, the trustees, the pastors who had come to visit me, and no telling how many others from over the years—these were just beginning to be answered by the One who never forgets.

A couple of weeks after the man passed away, my stepdaughter said, "Daddy, will you take me to this event where a bunch of dads are taking their daughters?"

"What kind of event is it?"

"It's a Christian event downtown in the basement of the Life-Way building."

Gulp. "Baby, I don't think so."

She insisted. I objected. We did this song and dance for a couple of days, but her pleading only grew in intensity, complete with tear-filled doe eyes and all the other things that would cause even a hardened criminal to melt under the pressure of the bright lights of her interrogation.

I finally gave in with caveats. "Okay, okay. I'll go on one condition. I drop you off and sit in the car outside the building. When you get done, you can come back in the car and we'll leave."

She thought for a moment. "Okay, Daddy," she said with a little mischievous grin.

The LifeWay building was located off Demonbreun Street on the East side of Interstate 40, right in the heart of downtown. I knew it very well. Many years later, it was razed to the ground and a new one was built down near Charlotte Avenue. But in my mind, if I were to walk into that headquarters for so many things Jesus- and church-related, it would crumble to the ground on its own simply because it wouldn't be able to contain a hypocrite like me.

The big day finally arrived, and I drove her downtown. I pulled up outside the building and put the car in park. There was a huge cross on the side of the building that had my full attention … as you know, I have some history with crosses. I felt so uncomfortable that my hands were literally shaking with nervousness as I gripped the steering wheel. Of course, kids don't always notice what's happening to those around them, especially when they're excited.

"Daddy, you have to come inside with me!" my step-daughter said.

I was no fool. There was no doubt that this was her scheme from the beginning, which I had suspected and which also probably explained why I was already so very nervous.

"No. That was not the deal, honey."

She was no fool either, always two steps ahead of me. The tears came, which I was somewhat ready for, but I was not ready for what came next. "All the girls are going to be with their daddies in there, and my real dad isn't here."

Her dagger hit its mark. The next thing I knew, she was dragging me by the hand into the building. I had insisted that we weren't staying for long, but we both knew that my protests were now merely for show. I had taken down some big dudes in prison, but this ten-year-old girl had whipped me.

The basement level of the building was set up like a full-fledged venue. The event was a breakfast for dads and daughters, so people were everywhere. There was also a huge stage where a Christian band was going to play for everyone after we ate. I didn't just feel like a fish out of water; imagine if someone asked that fish to also carry a briefcase and make a PowerPoint presentation.

When we sat down to eat, I felt like such a phony. I knew I was an evil man who had been miraculously rescued but who had drifted far. They had no idea who they were eating with, but these "normal" Christian dads just talked to me as if I was like them. I mostly just nodded my head and tried not to embarrass my stepdaughter, but inside, I was worried that my evil was somehow going to spill out on everyone.

There was food in front of me, but I wasn't touching it. I had no appetite. But my little stepdaughter was so sweetly concerned for me that she insisted I eat. Since she was obviously in charge at that point, I took a few bites. I think it really helped to calm my nerves enough to not just crawl out of my own skin.

Next, the band took the stage. I had no idea what a huge moment this would end up being in my life. I didn't even know that Christian bands existed, so this was definitely the first time I had ever heard one. If you had asked me what I thought a Christian band would sound like, I can promise you it wouldn't have been this. They weren't cheesy and awful … they were actually really solid musicians and singers. I was impressed.

Finally, a pastor stood up to talk to us after the concert. I had been to church the one time when the guy gave me the Bible, but I hadn't *really heard* a message in many, many years, probably since the days of listening to J. Vernon McGee on the radio in the work camp. It's hard to explain it, but this pastor's words sank deep into my heart. It was like one of those movies where someone finds a caveman frozen in ancient Siberian ice. Whatever it was inside me that was frozen in time from back in 1988 when I finished playing the part of Christ was beginning to come to life again. It felt like this pastor had a huge hammer and a chisel. The ice wasn't gone, but there were definitely major cracks forming.

I didn't raise my hand, go down front, or ever pray a prayer that day, but neither did I run out kicking and screaming. I still kind of wanted to at times, but there was no doubt that something had been reawakened within me, so much so that in the following weeks, I began attending church again.

Hard Endings and New Beginnings

My wife was furious that I was even exploring something related to faith. We argued about it, and since I was by no means a strong believer, I probably didn't fight very fair. I didn't show her the love of Christ that was being shown to me in a way that would have invited her to experience it, too. I was still very immature in the faith, barely able to take a breath myself.

Months passed, and as I crept back toward the anchor from which I had drifted, I drifted further away from my wife. She became distant and bitter toward me, and I'm sure I was much the same toward her. I could sense that she had already moved on in her heart. She became increasingly detached from our relationship. Against everything she believed in, I somehow even convinced her to go to counseling with me at the church where I was given the Bible. I honestly tried everything I thought was right in order to reconcile and salvage our relationship.

Even so, our marriage—my second one—was over.

The divorce was actually very amicable. It was as if we knew we were going in completely different directions, so we mutually agreed to part ways. I'm not saying it was the right decision, but she did not want to be married to me anymore and was already moving on with other men. Our lifestyles had diverged.

One of the hardest things I ever had to do was get down on my knees, look my stepdaughter in the eyes, and tell her that it was not her fault that we were separating. She cried, and I hugged her tightly, but I knew that I would probably not be in her life in the future—her mom was going a completely different direction. It broke my heart and continues to do so to this very day.

Neither my stepdaughter nor my stepson probably have any idea how much they meant to me. They probably don't know how much they played into how long I was able to try to stay married nor how much God used them to begin cracking the ice inside me. Later that year, I called my now ex-wife, asking her to forgive me for not being the man she needed me to be in her life. I told her I was sorry for all the things I didn't do as a father and a husband. There was a long pause on the other end, but then she said that, yes, she would forgive me. That gave me a little bit of peace, enough to move on to what was next in my life.

But the divorce certainly hit me hard. I was back at a place where I believed Christ, but it almost put me back into a state of constant disappointment in myself. To believe in Jesus and what He cares about meant that I had to care about the same things. For years, I had decided not to carry the weight of caring—to just be and let the past fade away. But it hadn't worked. I couldn't escape what I knew to be the truth.

After the divorce, I gave up on trying to make it in Nashville. It was time to stop running and go home. I had learned so much during my time in Nashville about the way the music industry works. I had gained an understanding of songwriting, publishing, and event management. These lessons and skills seemed wasted at the time, but they would prove to be a very important part of my future. God wasn't about to waste anything from my past, no matter how wastefully this prodigal insisted on living.

The other thing was that I had found work in a new field: computers, specifically networking. I had secured a job for a major computer company in Nashville (which shall remain nameless). As was my custom, I just left the background check section of their application blank. For whatever reason, it worked, and I was hired. I regret doing this because a half lie is still a lie, so I hate that I misled them. However, I am grateful that I was able to learn so much from the experience.

I found out that I had a propensity for networking and troubleshooting technical issues. It was behind-the-scenes work, so it was perfect for a guy who wanted to avoid the spotlight. I also loved that I was able to help people solve their problems. I was actually able to contribute. I threw myself into this work, taking every class I could on the side that would add more certifications and skill sets to my portfolio.

In 2006, I moved back to Winchester as TJ Stevens, the network engineer. I moved into my dad's old guesthouse, which was actually a pole barn up on a small mountain. I was technically a man of faith again—but I again felt the need to hide. Two failed marriages were in my rearview mirror, so my confidence about what might lie ahead was low. Therefore, laying low, working hard, and keeping to myself seemed to make the most sense to me at the time.

Since I had some experience and certifications in the networking world, I applied at a hospital system for a tech job. As usual, I left the questions about any past convictions blank and just hoped for the best. This time, it did not go my way. They obviously performed the background check anyway and politely informed me that because of my ten counts of various offenses, include the use of a firearm to commit a crime, they simply could not hire me. I wasn't angry at them—I agreed with them. That was who I was, so I knew that it couldn't always be avoided.

But this did mean that I missed out on a pretty solid paycheck. I was finally able to secure a job working for a small computer company for eight dollars an hour. It was a start, but it wasn't enough. In the long run, not getting the job I wanted was probably one of the best things that ever happened to me because it led me to something better in the future.

As I worked for this low wage, I kept applying elsewhere, but no one wanted to hire me. It was hard to face this rejection, but it helped to refine what I really wanted. I wanted to be able to sustain myself, not being dependent upon others. The desire was not coming out of a place of anger or isolation but from a place of growth and maturity. It was time. Eventually, I launched out and started my own company—the one I still own and manage today.

Up The Mountain

I had some solitude up on my little mountain, especially when I started working for myself. It had both healthy and unhealthy aspects, but I think it was good for me just to get grounded in a place far away from the chasing of so many fleeting things that had characterized my life back in Nashville. I certainly missed my stepchildren and thought of them often, but it was also very nice to be closer to my own kids.

Besides my kids, however, I wasn't a big fan of visitors. I've never quite lost the cautious feeling that someone will come for me to punish me for my past crimes. I've lived a lot of my life feeling like Shrek: an ogre living in a swamp just waiting for mobs with pitchforks to attack and pillage.

One day, an old Jeep came rambling up the mountain and into my driveway. It caught my attention for sure. A guy got out and came up to my door. I opened the door and looked at him through the screen.

"Hey, there," he said, "I'm Mike Price. I'm a pastor, and, um, I would really would love to have you come to our church and sing."

His request made me mad for some reason … I guess I was still partially frozen. I went off on him.

"Who do you think you are coming up here? You shouldn't be on this property—you're trespassing!"

He got the point and quickly got back into his Jeep to drive back down the mountain. That was that.

Until the next week when he came back up again.

Mike was about ten years younger than I was, and I got the impression that he knew some things about me, but I couldn't tell how much. I wasn't about to volunteer any extra information. He obviously knew I could sing, which I assumed meant he had seen me perform back before I moved to Nashville and was doing some events around Winchester.

I yelled at him again before he could even get any words out, so he left again. Another week passed, and he drove up again. This time, I walked out into the front yard, which, again, was surrounded by woods. I guess I made him nervous, for good reason, because he started backing up and said, "Hey, you don't know who I am, do you?"

"No," I said. "I don't recognize you at all. "

He continued, "I met you back in 1985 when I was sixteen years old. You came to my church down in Sterling. You were wearing a white suit, and you sang a song called 'Basics of Life' to our entire congregation. I was in the youth group."

I didn't recall anything he was talking about at first, but when he mentioned it, it all began to come back to me. When I was meeting with the group at Rita's house, I had gone a few places to sing, including that church in Sterling. Mike was just a kid back then, but he remembered me. He said that when I sang that song, it really made a difference in his life. He knew I had just gotten out of prison at the time, though he didn't know for what.

I softened up a bit at the mention of those days at Rita's house. "I'm sorry, but I don't live that life anymore, man. Nobody wants me in their church. If I go to your church, they might as well just burn it to the ground."

But just like so many other people in my life, Mike refused to get lost in my smokescreen—he muscled through it. "Come on, man … you've got to come sing just one song. Just sing the song, and you can leave right afterward."

I didn't say yes, but I didn't say no either. He came up the mountain a few more times until I finally gave in, agreeing to sing *just* one song. When I showed up, I found that Mike's new church—called Church of the Valley—was meeting in a tent in the backwoods of Middletown, Virginia. But they had a stage and a sound system, so I fulfilled my obligation and sang the one song. Then Pastor Jay Ahlemann gave a message on forgiveness and grace.

It felt good, much better than I anticipated. There were no pitchforks or mobs. The people were grateful and accepting. It felt so right, in fact, that I showed up the next week, and then the next. I eventually became a member of the church and one of the musicians on their worship team. I hadn't yet told them all the full story of my past, but I fully rededicated my life to Christ during this time. I began developing relationships in the church and serving as much as possible.

Eventually, I started a Christian band, something I hadn't even known existed a few years before. I wrote songs about Jesus, and we performed them at churches all across the Shenandoah Valley. Pastor Mike continued to be a key catalyst and an encouragement in pushing me toward serving Christ and other people.

That little church became my community. Out of those relationships, I began to grow as a disciple. I also met the love of my life that same year. She was a dancer at a theater where we were doing a benefit. She also went to the same church. This time, the wife I married was a fully committed Christian, as was I, which meant we were both more prepared to face the challenges of marriage completely dependent upon Christ. She knew about my past but kept it a secret between us. I couldn't believe that someone could love me so honestly, but God was restoring all the things I had once squandered.

I am forever indebted to Mike Price for pursuing me. He was a longtime friend who never gave up on me and whom God used mightily to show me grace and spur me along to love and good works. Later, Mike started making a documentary about my life, but it was cut short when he passed away in 2016. I miss him, but his life and his legacy are eternal.

CHAPTER 12

From Hiding to Sharing

I had moved out of the shadows in my personal life and faith, but I was definitely still hiding my story back in the dark. I would have been more than content to live the rest of my life in this state—experiencing the safety of my renewed life in Christ, a healthy marriage, and a thriving Christian community.

I bet Joseph felt something similar during the years he spent between prison and his brothers' arrival. He had a new identity, complete with everything he needed to live a healthy, fulfilled life—a wife, kids, a great job, the respect of his community. But then, one day, he had to face his past. He had to come clean about how he got there.

God did the same thing in me. He wasn't going to let me just live in the security of what He had done in me. He wanted me to share it with others. Some people love to talk about themselves. I actually hate it. This is not because I am extra humble or more spiritual; it is because when I look backward, it is hard to face who I was and what I did. Paul even references this feeling in Romans 6:21 (NLT) when he asks those who once lived in shadows but now resided in the light: "And what was the result? You are now ashamed of the things you used to do, things that end in eternal doom."

But through a divine process, God began pushing me toward not just accepting His grace and forgiveness but also accepting His healing for the wounds of shame in my heart. No, there will never be a moment in my life when I am just "okay" with what I did. However, God has spent years helping me see that my identity is no longer that troubled young man.

I am no longer Jamie Stevens, the school shooter. I am TJ Stevens, once a shooter, but now clothed and in his right mind. Like Paul, who was once a killer, I can talk about what I did back then in my old identity. I can even own the *fault* of it, but the *weight* of it has been carried by Christ. The shame of my old life crushed Him on the cross so that I don't have to be crushed by its weight anymore. Yes, I am responsible, but my sentence has been served by another. Thus I am free—not to continue in such foolish, destructive patterns, but truly free to live the life I could never find on my own.

Is it fair that I am free? No. It is not fairness … it is grace.

I took years to get here, and it is a journey I'm still on every day, but becoming healthy in my relationships with God and His people were huge beginnings. As my band began playing in more and more places across Virginia, it became evident that God had more than just those beginnings in mind. I also began organizing and promoting Christian events during this time, something about which I will share more soon. But regardless of what I was doing, it was obvious that I couldn't just stay where everything was comfortable.

God brought it all to a head in 2011. A pastor named Andy Combs, a guy I barely knew, booked my band to play for a Saturday night service for youth. That night, something went haywire with the speaker he had booked, and long story short, there was no one available to fill in.

We were backstage with Andy, who was having quite the freak-out moment. He turned to me and said, "Hey, man, we're in a real situation here. Can you give your testimony after you guys play?"

Silence.

"Um, dude," I finally said. "That's not going to happen."

That wasn't going to cut it for Andy, who gave me quite the curious look. "You mean to tell me that you're out here singing songs about Jesus and all the things He does in people's lives, but you can't even share for a few minutes about what He's done in your own life?"

Ouch.

My heart began to race. "Listen, dude, I get it. I should be doing something like that, but you don't know me."

It became obvious that Andy wasn't going to let it go, so I asked him to meet me outside at the back of the building. He probably wondered if I was going to try to fight him, but I just wanted to speak with him privately.

"Now listen," I said solemnly. "You've got kids in there, and my testimony consists of three things: a high-powered rifle, a high school, and hostages."

That was the most I had ever shared with anyone outside my family. I figured that just a little detail about exactly how screwed up my story was would do the trick to deter his relentless pursuit.

Andy was silent for a long moment.

Then he shocked me by saying, "Cool!"

I almost fell down. "Wait, dude, what? I thought you're going to tell me to pack up my stuff and get out of the building!"

He just looked at me and smiled. "No, man. You mean you got a story like *that* and now you're here singing for Jesus? That's unbelievable!"

I was shocked. "Well, yeah … I guess that's kind of … the gist of the whole deal."

"You should share, TJ."

"No, I'm no hero … I am a coward. And I don't want to hurt those kids in there. I've hurt kids before."

Finally, he could tell that I simply wasn't ready to do it that night, so he let it go. But that conversation awakened something within me. It made my spirit start looking in a different direction. I started questioning everything I was doing—that is, going to church every Sunday and playing the part of a guy in a Christian band but not really revealing all that Christ had done in me. My heart was challenged.

This was the first time I'd ever really been confronted about telling my story publicly. Back in 2009, I actually broke down and secretly shared my story with a few friends, Michelle and Aaron Milbourne, after a long praise and worship practice at church. We stayed and talked past one o'clock in the morning, sitting in low light on the back row of an empty church in Strasburg. I remember shaking as I told them. Their response was so encouraging. They said they both knew I was carrying the weight of something major, and they promised to keep it secret. They encouraged me to share it publicly as well, but they didn't push me quite the way that Andy did.

Little seeds like these conversations let me know that God was serious about me sharing. And what began as a fluke led to Pastor Andy's relentless passion for me to share. He just wouldn't let it go. For the next two years, he constantly and lovingly challenged and encouraged me to speak out. I ran from it. I talked myself out of it. I tried to convince myself I was protecting the people around me. But every time I would take ground in my mind, God would conquer yet another acre of my resistance.

Finally, two years later, I broke the silence. Appropriately, it happened at Andy's church, What's New Worship in Winchester, which was gathering in the meeting room of a Travelodge at the time. About ninety people showed up. Andy stood up and introduced me. He still did not know everything I was going to say. He just told them he knew my story was going to be incredible.

I had vomited in the bathroom before taking the stage. I was shaking, but I knew this was right. I had written everything down to keep myself from freaking out or losing my place.

There were many people in the crowd with whom I had attended church and built relationships for the past several years. I feared I would lose all my friends as well as my jobs—both as the owner of a networking company and a promoter for bands. Who was going to want to hire a guy who was once a shooter?

But I stood there, opened my mouth, and told them an amended version of the story contained in these pages. I started in the bedroom with my rifle. I told them about the voices. The big coat. The shooting. The hostages. The hand. The change.

You could have heard a pin drop. People immediately began *looking down* so they could *look up* my story on their phones to see if it was legit. It was. Then they locked their eyes on me as I muddled my way through what Jesus had done for me. It wasn't polished, but I guess it didn't need to be. I tried to keep it as "PG" as possible since there were kids in the room, but the general story still seemed to capture everyone's full attention.

When it was over, people lined up to talk to me. They didn't reject me; they loved me. I heard "we never knew" over and over again, but not in a tone of condemnation. Several people prayed to accept Christ in their lives that Sunday morning in that hotel meeting room.

I walked away from that night completely floored. The very thing I had run away from—the story I was so ashamed of that I thought would cost me everything—was proving to be the very strength of my life and the one thing that God could most use to rescue other people.

REACHING MORE PEOPLE

As I mentioned, during that season, I also began the journey toward becoming a Christian event promoter. The seed that was planted in me that morning in the LifeWay building was now springing out of the ground and bearing fruit in my life. I was an eyewitness to the power of music to heal and break down barriers in people's lives, so I began helping to organize events with the hope that it might do the same for others.

It really felt like God was leading me to do this kind of work. As my heart had been opened to the light of living life with God and His people, I was more willing to make myself available. This was also the moment when everything I learned about the music industry, agents, radio promoters, and live events came to bear on my future. I just took those lessons and applied them to this new endeavor. God had truly prepared me.

One of the first concerts I ever did was a fundraiser for a little girl named Reagan, who had cancer. I felt so energized not only to be raising money but also to be raising awareness and fostering a sense of community, love, and concern for someone in great need. It was the beginning of many new things, which included not only planning and promoting the event, but also my personal communication with agents, staff, artists, and volunteers. I had come so far that I often found myself surrounded by hundreds of volunteers as I encouraged them not only to do their best that night but to remember that this event was for an audience of One.

I was actually leading.

The events grew in scope and success much more quickly than I ever thought they could. The expenses for the first one were only $7,000. My second event doubled to $14,000, while the third jumped to $35,000. I was blown away. I had always felt like an outcast, but now churches, event organizers, and radio stations were trying to associate themselves with me because we were pulling off the best events around.

Things grew so fast that I had to stop and do a lot of soul searching early on. Was I doing all this for the right reasons? Was I trying to prove to myself or to others that I wasn't worthless or that I could be successful? God really worked on my heart during this season, and sometimes it was painful as I dealt with my own pride and insecurity. But He continues to be faithful to refine me when I lose sight of what's really happening, turning and constantly returning me to a place where I once again remember that these events have one purpose: to seek those who, like me, don't yet know that God loves them and is more than willing to transform their lives by His grace.

I have many memories of incredible things happening at these events, but one sticks out above the rest. We were hosting Big Daddy Weave for a huge concert. At the end, Mike Weaver, the lead singer and front man, invited anyone who wanted to respond to Christ's offer of grace to come forward and pray with the volunteers. I stood there at an event I had organized and watched as hundreds and hundreds of people came forward.

I became overwhelmed with emotion, and I heard a whisper in my heart: "This is why I let you live." Though I had shared it a few times, most of the people who had bought tickets had no clue about my story. In that moment, it didn't matter. It was as if I could feel the culmination of everything from 1982 through 2015—so much of what had gone wrong being redeemed before my very eyes for a higher, eternal purpose.

Another time, I received a phone call from a lady in Fairfax who told me about her friend with cancer. Her doctors said she probably only had about three months to live. We were about to put on a huge concert with Jason Gray and Plumb. She wanted to know if there was any way I could get her a personal meet-and-greet with Tiffany Arbuckle from Plumb.

At the time, we had an event before the concert called "Breakfast With Plumb" where fans could pay extra money to meet the band. They could also pay even more money to get to see Tiffany's bus and meet her. For a moment, I was calculating all the costs and logistics when I suddenly came to my senses. "I'm going to make it happen for you," I said matter-of-factly. I told her to meet me backstage at a certain time.

The night of the concert, the woman who called me showed up with her friend, who was quite pale and weak. She was wearing a "do rag" on her head as a result of losing all her hair. She couldn't have been any older than mid- to late twenties. My heart broke for her.

We walked into the back parking lot, where people were already lined up at Tiffany's bus. "Just stay with me," I said. Honestly, I wasn't sure if it was going to work out or not. I didn't have tickets to show their management and security, and that was a problem. But just like so many times before in my life when I just applied for the job and didn't check the boxes, I just went for it.

The security guys knew I was the promoter, so they let me through, and I knocked on the bus door. Someone answered, and Tiffany was sitting near the front of the bus, so she could hear me.

"Hey, I have a friend here that needs to speak with you," I said. I didn't go into any details about her health.

Tiffany spoke up without hesitation. "Sure, TJ! Come on up."

Tiffany was so gracious, spending an hour with the young woman and her friend. Afterward, I took them to front-row seats for the show. At the end of the night, the woman was completely exhausted from all the excitement, but her deep, abiding gratitude rang out through her weak, raspy voice. There may have been thousands of people there that night, but I know God had that one young woman in mind when He decided to put me in the place where I could help organize those kinds of moments.

There are many other stories like this, each one just more evidence of grace that is still trickling down from a God who throws no one away—a Rescuer who desires to heal, redeem, and restore people from all walks of life, even people who walk far away from Him.

People like me.

FULL CIRCLES

As we near the end of these pages, I want to be clear that I am nowhere near the end of my story. I haven't arrived at perfection. I haven't conquered every temptation or achieved some superior level of spirituality. I don't deserve what I've been given, and I have never stopped being surprised by grace.

Grace just keeps going.

Who I am in Christ today is so vastly different from whom I was without Him back then. I used to see myself only as a worthless failure, but today, He keeps revealing over and over again that He sees me as a son. Just this morning, I was sitting under a tree reading from the book of John—and sure enough, the passage I was reading happened to be about another guy whom Jesus saw sitting under a tree long before they ever met.

As I enjoyed this quiet moment with my Savior over a cup of coffee, it was just another of a million reminders that He sees me … that He has always seen me. We are prone to believe that God only sees us in our worst moments, but now that I know I am His son, I am learning that He has seen me in every moment. This shift in identity from hiding into abiding with Him is something I never could have earned or produced on my own.

But as I said, grace just keeps going … and this means that I just keep growing into my new identity in Christ. Though it has had incredible moments—even miraculous ones—it has been a steady change produced by living alongside a lot of steady people. God has walked with me, even when I didn't know He was there. He has been faithful to work in me, even when I have been far from faithful.

And along the way, my identity, including how I see myself, continues to morph and reflect how He sees me instead.

He even graciously allowed my legal status to reflect these internal changes when in 2016, I received an executive order from the governor of Virginia that restored my rights as a citizen to vote, hold office, be a notary public, and serve on a jury. The only restriction that it did not remove was the right to own a firearm, which is something I have no interest in doing anyway. The first time I went to vote in the next election, let's just say that the registration process was complicated— it's not every day that a former school shooter walks in to vote carrying an executive order allowing him to do so. This is just another example of how God has chosen to graciously restore me in so many ways that never seemed even remotely possible.

Up to this point, my story has been about an active, merciful Savior reaching out His hand to me both directly and through people. As we face the onslaught of school shootings, violence, racism, and other social evils today, my hope is that each of us will find the same hope that found me.

You may be someone's Rita Warren—a person with a vision to tell the story of Jesus and a willingness to listen to God's direction, dismissing and disqualifying no one from helping that story be told. To this day, I don't know if Rita ever knew about my past. She may have passed away by now, so I'm not sure. Back around 2013 when I first began to share it, I tracked down her phone number and called her.

"This is James," I said, "the young man who played the part of Jesus."

She immediately began crying, her love for me still so strong. We caught up for a few minutes, and I started to tell her about my real story, but I decided against it—not out of shame, but more from a desire not to overwhelm or burden her at that stage of her life. She had never before cared where I had been or what I had done, so I just focused on her and what was going on in her life. She had written a book about our adventures doing the Passion play, and she sent me a signed copy.

You may be someone's Don Grant, the SWAT negotiator who became my lifeline. Back in 2012 when I was living by myself up on the mountain in Winchester, I prayed that God would let me meet Don again someday. About two years later, I got the strangest phone call from my dad.

He started off by telling me that I wasn't going to believe who he had just got off the phone with. It was my Uncle Corky, who lived in Florida. He was playing golf with a guy who used to be a hostage negotiator in Virginia. After this seemingly chance meeting, they had put two and two together because of my uncle's last name: Stevens. The golfer was Don. He said he remembered me well and wanted to know if I ever wanted to talk to him.

My heart hit the floor. About three weeks later, I got a phone call from Don. The last time I had heard his voice over the phone was the day I almost murdered myself and many others. Just like that fateful day, he called me Jamie.

I began pouring out everything inside me. I thanked him over and over again. I told him that I have kids and grandkids now, and that I am organizing events that give people hope and life instead of darkness and death. I told him about all the police conventions and events that I speak at and all the ways those heroes respond to me with kindness and empathy. I told him that whatever else he did in his career before he retired, he had made the difference between life and death for me. Since then, we talk on the phone about every six months or just shoot a text to each other to check up on what's happening.

We still have plans to get that beer if he ever makes it up this way or vice versa.

You may be one of the teachers or administrators who found themselves being held hostage by a madman but who still had the wherewithal to show compassion to their attacker. You know how my hostages tried to persuade me not to hurt myself, which would have ended their immediate danger. But what you probably don't know is the way that some of the other people who were in the school that day have offered me mercy and compassion years later.

When I first began sharing my story, I was speaking in a church on a Sunday morning. Directly afterward, a young lady approached me and said, "I've heard this story my whole life."

"What do you mean?" I asked.

"My mom was there that day in the school."

But she wasn't just present during the shooting years before; she was actually there *in the church* that morning—and her daughter introduced us. All I could do was beg for her forgiveness because I couldn't imagine the trauma and fear I had inflicted upon her young life at the time, things she had to carry with her all these years.

She looked me in the eyes and told me that Christ had forgiven her, so she was happy to forgive me as well. The pastor of the church saw this happening and asked her if she would share in the second service. She said yes. So after I spoke, she came up on the stage and we shared our brand-new story with everyone there—and she told me on the stage in front of everyone watching that she forgave me.

There wasn't a dry eye in the building. That kind of reckless, Christlike compassion wrecked me in the best possible way. Consequently, people lined up that day to accept the invitation to know the kind of God who would orchestrate something so beautiful in broken people's lives. Who wouldn't want that kind of love?

I experienced another life-changing expression of grace when I met Beth Nimmo, the mother of seventeen-year-old Rachel Scott, one of the victims of the Columbine shooting. We actually recorded an *I Am Second* video together. Quite honestly, how could a mother who had lost so much sit across from a man who had committed similar actions as the ones who had taken her daughter from her?

Despite her loss, she spoke to me with such grace. People sometimes speak of sensing that God's presence is near, which can sound mysterious and kooky. But in that atmosphere where such potential pain was being displaced by such unspeakable mercy, we all felt that God's own Spirit was literally resting on the room. It's no surprise that such a presence would be felt where people were treating other people like Jesus treats people.

So for you, I humbly offer up the only hope I have found in my own life. The issues we are facing today are beyond serious, and I know I cannot solve them in a few hundred pages. What I can do, however, is not hide … not hide the monster that I became, nor the redemption that transformed me into someone else altogether. My past may influence me, but it cannot define me. I am not my past, and Christ now holds my future.

Believe what you may, but I am convinced there is a spiritual enemy who wants to steal from us, kill us, and ultimately destroy everything and everyone we love. I know it's easier to chalk up such a belief to fundamentalist froth, but I beg you to hear me: I have felt his darkness. He is a smart adversary. Think about it: if you were smart, wouldn't you have much to gain from convincing the world at large that you don't really exist outside of cartoons and movies where you carry a pitchfork and have a pointy tail?

Sounds like a brilliant strategy to me.

What do we do with this concept of a spiritual enemy? First of all, I think it is important to acknowledge the spiritual component of this whole issue instead of just boiling it down to anything else we can find. Yes, bullying is a component. Yes, mental health is absolutely a component and should be an area where we seek better treatment and identify potential dangers long before those suffering from it escalate to violence.

To that end, I really don't think any of us can determine the exact dividing line between mental health and spiritual darkness. I don't think violent acts are always the sole result of one or the other. In general, from a biblical worldview, all violence and destruction of valuable life is the result of our spiritual enemy, Satan, working in and among us. This doesn't necessarily mean that "the devil makes us do it," but there is a general struggle—a vying for control and influence over us all.

In terms of mental illness, I think those who struggle with it, which is something no one should be ashamed of, may be easier targets for spiritual attacks, just as someone with asthma is more susceptible to altitude sickness. To be clear, we are all susceptible to making mistakes or even committing crimes; my point is that if someone is already struggling with chemical imbalances or even the trauma of violence or abuse in their past, they may be an easier target for the enemy to pick on. It may be helpful for us to not always treat psychology and spirituality as if they are polar opposites of each other. Researchers and psychologists like Carl Jung have acknowledged the critical connection between psychological problems and spiritual problems. As much as we want to downplay or dismiss the spiritual, it won't just go away—mainly because it is actually real.

My hope and encouragement to you is that we will love those around us well—and especially those who seem to be struggling in psychological as well as spiritual areas. May we not isolate them, ostracize them, or treat them as less than anyone else.

I was the lesser one, so I know how this feels.

I encourage you to pay attention to kids and young adults who seem to be isolating themselves or lashing out more than usual. Don't just correct them—listen to them! Remind them that they are valuable not just to God but also to you. Dig deeper to make sure they aren't facing neglect or abuse. I wish someone would have dug deeper for me.

Show them love, even if they don't seem very lovable. It may not be what they say they want, but it is most definitely what they need, and you can always choose to give it.

It is no secret at this point that I believe our only hope in this life is found in the grace of Christ. I also believe this grace is our only hope for someday seeing the senseless acts of violence against our children come to a halt. This may not be a popular opinion in every social or political circle these days, but would it be better for me to alter the truth of my story to avoid publishing an unpopular conclusion? What I'm saying is that I have actually experienced something more real than just mere religion, church attendance, emotionalism, or piety.

I experienced real Love that found me in my darkest moment, offered me rescue, and never stopped pursuing me. And He continues to do so even today. Why did He do this for me? Trust me, it wasn't so someone would think He only cares for certain people. He wanted me to be another one of His infinite examples of what He can do with nothing. He created the world out of nothing. He created man from a pile of dirt.

I was a pile of dirt too … but now I'm alive. So no matter how low, dirty, or worthless you think you are, I invite you to look at my life and think again.

I have never again physically seen the hand that appeared to me that day in the school, but I still see it all the time in my life. It doesn't have to be seen with physical eyes to be recognized and reached for. In fact, it is reaching out for you, just as it did for me.

Just take it.

Epilogue

I sometimes find it ironic—in a good way—that as someone whose story begins by opening fire in his school, I've been asked many times over the last few years to share my testimony with schoolchildren.

The following letters are just a few of the many I've received that have touched my heart.

Dear T.J. Stevens,

Thank you so much for sharing your testimony. My name is [A.B.]. I'm in 7th grade, and my mom has breast cancer. Even though I was a little scared, your testimony made me want to share mine. We don't know what stage she is, but I know God has her in His hands.

Have a good one,
A.B.

Dear T.J.,

Thank you for coming out and giving us your
testimony. It showed me how God can change someone
and completely make them love God so much.

Sincerely,
 Chase

Dear T.J. Stevens,

Thank you for sharing your testimony with us.
It scared me at first. But soon, slowly, I discovered the
wonderful works of God. Your testimony definitely touched
me in a way that nothing else has ever touched me in my
life. I thank you for coming the length that you went to
share your testimony. I'm really glad that you came.

Thank you.
Rachel M.

Dear T.J. Stevens,

Thank you so much for coming to tell your testimony to all of us. You have one of the best testimonies ever because God has done some awesome things in your life. Your testimony showed me that God loves everyone and He is there for everyone. So thank you for your time to come out and tell your testimony.

Love,
Mikayla

Acknowledgments

This book would not have been possible without the tre-
mendous love and support of more people than I could
ever name. To that end, this list does not reflect everyone who
has been instrumental in my journey, but I do want to mention a few.

To my mom, my stepmother, and father: your love and
support in all my endeavors has been endless. You continue
to guide me in becoming the man God created me to be. I love
you all. To my grandfather after whom I was named: you
taught me later in life that it's never too late to do the right
thing. To my children and grandchildren, my brothers—
Bobby, Eddie, Tony, Andy, and Jordie—and to my extended
family on both sides: your love and support have been felt all
my life. Finally, to my wife, Krista: you are my best friend and
my constant source of encouragement in all things. Your love
and prayers have been the gentle tools of God's most amazing
work in my life.

As I continue this journey, there have been so many divine
appointments that I will never take for granted. Each is a crucial part of the elevation of my story and what God has chosen
to do with it.

Pastor Andy Combs, thank you for calling me out and challenging my spirit by your first request to speak to others about what Jesus has done for me. God surely used you to pull that dusty car cover off the hidden gift of life I was refusing to acknowledge. The entire congregation of What's New Worship, thank for your constant encouragement, acceptance, and prayer.

Justin Moyer, the *Washington Post* journalist whose research and persistence found me at the time, thank you for having the initiative to look beyond the person everyone thought I was and to understand what really changed me.

Marji Ross, Tim Peterson, and the incredible publishing team at Regnery and Salem Books: thank you for taking a chance on this story and for equipping me to tell more people about the blindingly bright love of God that found me in my darkest moment.

My incomparable literary agents, Robert Wolgemuth and Austin Wilson, as well as my collaborative writer who partnered with me in getting the right words onto the page: I am so grateful for all the support, time, and energy you have put into me and into this project.

And finally, let me just list many more people who fall into many more categories, including friends, editors, filmmakers, coworkers, ministry leaders, producers, artist representatives, journalists, and more. The list may be long, but my humble gratitude to each of you is much bigger—Christina Combs, Robert Amaya, Kristina Simpson, Lynn Tasker, the late Pastor Mike Price, the late Dale Allen, the Garland family, Jeremy Pommerening, David Ehrenberg, Carolyn McCulley, Lance

Villio, John Humphrey, Elizabeth Nimmo, Carolyn McCready, Tom DeKorne, Jessica Fry, John and Lisa Wiles, Aaron and Michelle Milburn, the Ahlemann family, Evangelist Miguel Escobar, Pastors Chuck and Sheila Brown, Pastor Bradley Hill, Kialeen Potterton, Andrew Ward, Pat Harris, Bette Anderson, the Athey family, the Cullers family, Frank Paige, David Roy, Don Grant, Jim Pierce, the Dillow family, the Swartz family, the Spangler family, the Edwards family, Judy Wilfong, Lindsay E., Mark M., John and Cindy Mongold, Phil and Donna Hunt, Cookie Oats, Betsy Sibert, and Lisa Meadows. To each of you and many more, I offer my eternal gratitude— and obviously, true eternal gratitude goes to my Lord Jesus Christ, who completely rescued me both for this life and the one to come.

End Notes

Chapter 3: What (And Why) Now?

[1] Hebrews 11:1

[2] Dallas Willard, *The Divine Conspiracy: Rediscovering Our Hidden Life in God* (New York: HarperCollins Publishers, 1997), 79.

Chapter 7: Minimal Security

[1] The phrase "the freedom of self-forgetfulness" was coined by Tim Keller. His book by the same title delves deeper into this subject.